New Issues in Mediating the Israel-Palestine Deadlock

New Issues in Mediating the Israel-Palestine Deadlock

Edited by

Barry H. Steiner

BRILL
NIJHOFF

LEIDEN | BOSTON

Originally published, in part, as Volume 23, No. 1 (2018) of Brill Nijhoff's journal *International Negotiation*.

Cover illustration: U.S. Secretary of State John Kerry, Israeli Justice Minister Tzipi Livni, and Palestinian Chief Negotiator Saeb Erekat address reporters on the Middle East Peace Process Talks at the U.S. Department of State in Washington, D.C., on July 30, 2013. [State Department photo/ Public Domain].

Library of Congress Control Number: 2018967026

Typeface for the Latin, Greek, and Cyrillic scripts: "Brill". See and download: brill.com/brill-typeface.

ISBN 978-90-04-39328-8 (paperback)
ISBN 978-90-04-39329-5 (e-book)

This book is printed on acid-free paper and produced in a sustainable manner.

Contents

New Elements for Introducing Symmetry in the Middle East Peace Process

I. William Zartman
Nitze School of Advanced International Studies, The Johns Hopkins University, 1740 Massachusetts Avenue, Washington, DC 20036, USA
zartman@jhu.edu

Received 28 August 2017; accepted 6 September 2017

Abstract

This issue contains an examination of Palestinian-Israeli negotiations with an effort to break through the deadlock strategically. It analyzes the past record of failure and addresses the basic problem of asymmetry. Despite the solutions that have been advanced for all the specific issues, it is the forward-looking matter of trust that is the impediment to productive negotiations. The declaration of a Palestinian state and its recognition by the international community are now the basic elements necessary to break the asymmetry of the parties. A second element – allegedly favored by the Trump administration – is to reduce a symmetry by enlarging the playing field to include surrounding states, as proposed in the 2002 Arab Peace Initiative.

Keywords

negotiation – asymmetry – unilateral declaration of independence – trust – forward-looking negotiations – Arab Peace Initiative – recognition – Israel – Palestine

* I. William Zartman is the Jacob Blaustein Distinguished Professor Emeritus of International Organization and Conflict Resolution at the Nitze School of Advanced International Studies (SAIS), The Johns Hopkins University. He specializes in negotiation and conflict management, with particular attention to Africa and the Middle East.

 | DOI:10.1163/9789004393295_002

This is doubtless an unusual issue of *International Negotiation*, although it shouldn't be. It contains not only analyses of past negotiations and lessons from them, but also proposals for doing better next time. It is also a most appropriate issue, because next time is upon us. Repeated attempts at facilitating negotiations between Israel and Palestine have fallen into the sea because of the tactical assumption of symmetry under which hides the asymmetry of positions. This is a problem that the following four articles tackle, with both backward-looking and forward-looking analyses. At the same time, there is a change in the air, posited with the idea of enlarging the context and thereby the pie. An enlarged set of players can reduce the asymmetry problem, but by introducing new issues of interest to either side can it facilitate the resolution of the old issues that paralyzed earlier negotiations?

An Old Dilemma

The latest failure is analyzed by Amira Schiff in an examination of the Kerry Initiative, using three concepts that offer explanations for progress (or not) in negotiation. Ripeness theory identifies a necessary if insufficient condition for negotiations to begin, but in fact, its constituent subjective elements – a mutually hurting stalemate and a way out – are shown to be absent. Similarly, the push element of ripeness might be replaced by a pull element or at least augmented by its development during the negotiation, but that feature – a mutually enticing opportunity – was absent as well, both before and during the mediation effort. A structural rather than a processual concept – a central coalition – is also examined, although it does not explain why such a grouping can occur except through leadership (which goes back to the previous ideas). In any case, neither Kerry nor Israeli or Palestinian leaders were able to gather the necessary coalition across party divisions. That is where we are.

The other three articles attack the symmetry/asymmetry problem, the core of the issue. In a situation of asymmetrical power, Israel pursues a symmetrical strategy. From its administrative and security control of much of the Occupied Territory of the West Bank (and its security lock on Gaza), Israel frames negotiations as if the West Bank pie were being divided up, whereas it is rather a matter of deciding the borders of an already identified and UN-consecrated proto-state of Palestine. Galia Golan identifies the issues and obstacles, including the ambient political, psychological and emotional settings. As it turns out, most of the past issues – borders, security, Jerusalem, refugees, settlements – have already been handled a number of times with one or more solutions. It is rather the "forward" conditions of trust, reconciliation and implementation that keep the "backward" issues from being resolved (Zartman & Kremenyuk 2005).

To that, Barry Steiner says, "Go for broke!" To break the asymmetry, Palestine needs equal international standing and, for this, recognition of a Palestinian state is necessary. The longstanding US announcement in favor of a Palestinian state (inherent in a two-state solution) is old hat by now, in fact so old that that it being called into question in a search for alternatives. What is required now is recognition. Although this move might reify the stalemate at a higher level, it is the necessary condition for effective mediation, the article argues, and is a step toward bringing about an effective mutually hurting stalemate. However, recognition brings about another crucial aspect of the asymmetry: the fact that solid Israel-US relations are more important to both sides than a Palestinian solution. This could be worked both ways: it could be used to bring Israel along to a Palestine solution, but it has been used to hold the US back in its mediation *démarches*. The Peace Process is hostage to the Tel Aviv-Washington entente, which Washington has not been able to redirect (leadership problem again). Steiner sets up a decision tree after recognition, with the first branch focused on a change of Israeli government or not, and the dominant fallback to simply supporting the Palestinian moves on their own.

The asymmetry/symmetry problem is carried further by Walid Salem, extending the first notion by highlighting not only the asymmetrical legal status of the two parties but the creeping annexation that it allowed. Successive rounds of the Peace Process have served only to consolidate Israeli occupation of Palestine and turn occupation bit by bit into *de facto* annexation. The analysis introduces a new setting using international relations approaches. The asymmetry of past negotiations is grounded in the realist approach based on state power, and it treats the remaining 22 percent of the Palestine mandate territory as disputed territories and spoils of war to be divided between the two parties (of unequal standing). The transformative constructivist approach understands that the division has already taken place and the only remaining question is how to consolidate the 1967 borders and formalize relations. Under this approach, there are problems to be resolved between the two entities, but no longer the question of how to divide up the Palestinian territory. Measures include implementation of previous agreements, rebuilding Gaza and contacts with Hamas, supporting UN membership and economic reconstruction for Palestine, among others. The program means overcoming the asymmetry problem and taking Palestine seriously.

A final element in the process involves handling the problem of Hamas. As it stands, Hamas' positions on Israel are a barrier to its inclusion in a final settlement. But conditions do not just stand still and part of the process involves changing them. On one hand, the positions of Hamas have already evolved on matters such as a referendum and the 1967 boundaries, and indeed the very idea of *sulh* (truce) is more lasting than the position on current boundaries held by some of Israel's parties. On the other hand, an evolving process into a recognized state is more likely to bring in Hamas (kicking and screaming), rather than motivate it to stay outside as a spoiler. Similarly, in South Africa, Colombia and Burundi, among others, critical opposition parties joined the peace process when it appeared to bear fruit. Hamas needs to be brought in, not as a precondition, but as part of the process; the current split delays the process.

Resetting the Parties

The discussion can be expanded. The United States can begin by moving its embassy to Jerusalem. In fact, it can do more: it should move two embassies, by also setting up an embassy to a Palestinian state in East Jerusalem. Now that a new Administration has taken office in the US, there is a perfect opportunity for uniting two seemingly opposite policies and their supporters. The US can accede to the longstanding demand to put the embassy in the Israeli-proclaimed capital of their state, and at the same time can give concrete expression to its firmly announced two-state policy by recognizing the state of Palestine and putting the US embassy on the Palestinian side of the capital city. A real opportunity is open to change the stalemate and move the search for a Middle East problem ahead. It is time to recognize a Palestinian state and give it an embassy.

Negotiation concepts throw further light on the opportunity. All studies show that the more the parties make each other feel equal, the more productive the negotiations (Zartman & Rubin 2000). Currently, the asymmetry of the two parties, either formally or in power terms, is manifest. Israel has the edge by far in international legitimacy (recognition) and military strength. A change in the Palestinians' status would put the parties closer and on more equal terms, formally even if not in hard power. A promotion in status of the Palestine Liberation Organization (PLO) to the sole and legitimate representative of the Palestinian people was one of the elements that allowed an agreement to be concluded at Oslo in 1993 (even if not implemented), but after

over two decades of asymmetrical stalemate a further move toward equalizing status is necessary.

The time is now ready for the US to get out of its illogical contradiction, in which it declares a two-state situation as the solution but takes all action to block the second state that is half the solution. Admittedly, the full statement of US aims is "a two-state solution to be the result of negotiation between Israel and the Palestinian Authority (PA)." But as has been shown for years and repeatedly declared by Israeli Prime Minister Netanyahu, Israel will not negotiate, if negotiation is defined as a process of exchanging offers with the goal of reaching a mutually acceptable agreement. It thinks it is too strong to have to talk.

Another insight from negotiation analysis – and good sense – is that Israel will not move to give Palestine an independent existence as long as Tel Aviv is comfortable with the status quo. If it isn't broke, why fix it; if it doesn't hurt, why seek a cure? As long as occupation of the West Bank is not a liability, Israel has no incentive to lift the occupation. Recent moves of the PA, notably an appeal to the International Criminal Court (ICC), are designed to make it hurt and make occupation a liability. Fighting against occupation and for independence is an old tradition of US policy from its very beginning. In the past decades, freedom fighters and anti-colonial struggles (for which, the UN Security Council (UNSC) has resolved, violence is legitimate) have had US support, and during World War II resistance against Nazi occupation was encouraged by US policy and opinion. That approach and those values have been dropped. They need to be revived if we are to be faithful to ourselves.

For independence to be recognized, it must be declared, as it was in 1988 and recognized by the UN General Assembly in 2013. Unilateral declaration of independence (UDI) is also a strong tradition of US policy, again, from the very beginning when the US declared its independence from England. UDI is a common occurrence. It was practiced by European colonies in Africa and Asia after World War II and by the Soviet republics in connection with the collapse of the USSR. Israel achieved independent statehood upon UDI. Probably the most recent and most instructive case is that of Kosovo, which announced its UDI in 2008, recognized by the US, NATO allies and most other states.

UDI does not replace negotiation; it promotes it and is complemented by it. In all cases of UDI, negotiations then followed on a more equal basis between the new state and its former owner to settle remaining matters of detail and relations. Such negotiation can of course be very testy, since important items are left over to be settled, but they can also be straightforward, since settlement is in the interest of both parties. One matter is extremely important: the determination of boundaries. Unless boundaries are jointly decided, war between the independent parties is likely, as the cases of Eritrea, India, South Sudan, Algeria and others show, and the purpose of negotiation is to avoid war.

It needs to be emphasized that the measures of UDI and its recognition are not anti-Israeli and do not necessitate an anti-Israeli turn of US policy. The point is to rid Israel of a liability that it obviously cannot handle. Defense and protection of Israel needs to remain a constant commitment of US policy. That commitment was expressed by the US in the creation of Israel and also expressed in UN General Assembly Resolution 181 that provided for a Jewish – and an Arab – state. Moving the embassy to Jerusalem would be a reassuring action in response to pro-Israeli opinion, just as establishing an embassy for Palestine is an equalizing move in support of Palestinian demands. Beyond the legacy of historic relations of friendship, the commitment to Israel will still be necessary after Palestinian UDI and US recognition with an East Jerusalem embassy, simply because the current testy relations between Israel and its neighbors will take some time to become fully normalized. But the beginning of normal neighborly relations is the recognition of neighbors as states of equal status, freed of encroachment and occupation, with recognized and respected boundaries and US embassies in their capital.

Revising the Field

Attempts at negotiation to date have covered just about all the aspects of bilateral relations and individual state activities that could be used as tradeoffs for a comprehensive agreement. There is simply not enough yet uncovered that could be used to enlarge the pie and overcome the characteristic asymmetry. To do so would require going beyond bilateral relations and expanding the participants and the area involved. This possibility has currently risen to the fore in President Trump's comments on a new approach.

The Arab Peace Initiative (API) has engaged the countries of the Arab League since 2002. It was endorsed (unanimously with one reservation – Iran) by the Organization of Islamic Cooperation in 2003, reaffirmed in 2017, and is included in UNSC resolutions 1850 (2008) and 1860 (2009). It proposes trading full diplomatic relations with Israel in exchange for Israeli withdrawal to the 1967 lines, establishment of a Palestinian state on the formerly occupied territory, and "a just solution to the Palestinian refugee problem" involving voluntary return and compensation for non-returnees (UNGA resolution 194, 1948). It opens the Israel-Palestine negotiations to a larger set of players and therefore opens new tradeoffs.

As it is, Palestine has little to give Israel in exchange for a deal, other than relief from the burden and embarrassment of occupation. Rebellions usually form the basis of a deal of recognition in exchange for an end of violence. But as it is, Israel does not feel (or admit) a burden and embarrassment (or even an "occupation") and Palestine has generally given up violence some years ago. Arab states' entry into a peace agreement on API terms offers Israel peace and recognition, a significant new item of exchange; many Israelis have criticized their government for turning it down (Horowitz 2017). Obviously, the API includes the two-state solution and a right of return, details to be discussed and agreed upon.

Thinking regionally also opens possibilities of breaking out of two-state choices by opening up to other types of arrangements – a Palestinian-Jordanian confederation, an expanded Gaza to include northeast Sinai (Egypt), among others (Rusila 2017). It also would logically encourage a revival of the regional/functional solutions that began and ran aground as part of the peace movement of the 1970s. It might also provide a context that would help bring Hamas into the negotiations.

However, the field is not all that level. Although widely adopted, the Initiative is associated with Saudi Crown Prince Abdullah, and Saudi policies have been highly divisive in its campaign against Qatar and its rivalry with Iran, which earlier refused the Initiative. Thus, from the Arab side, a regional approach can well become a chessboard for playing out the current regional split, either as a Sunni (Saudi-Egyptian)-Shi'a (Iran- Syria-Iraq plus Qatar) dispute or a Saudi-Iran rivalry, one form or another of the Arab heartland against the Fertile (sometimes, fatal) Crescent. Though the tradeoff may not be unanimous on the Islamic side, it still provides a second element in the symmetrizing of the two sides, alongside the boost provided by the recognized independence of Palestine. If there is anything new to be found in a revived Peace Process, it is contained in these elements.

References

Horowitz, Nitzen (2017). "API-The Greatest Missed Opportunity in Israel's History." *The Jerusalem Post*, 25 April. Accessed at http://www.jpost.com/Opinion/Arab-Peace-Initiative-the-greatest-missed-opportunity-in-Israels-history-488952.

Rusila, Ari (2017). "Israel-Palestine Conflict: Regional Approach," March 8. Accessed at: https://arirusila.blogactiv.eu/2017/03/08/israel-palestine-conflict-regional-approach/.

Zartman, I. William and Jeffrey Rubin, editors (2002). *Power and Negotiation*. Ann Arbor: University of Michigan Press.

Zartman, I. William and Victor Kremenyuk, editors (2005). *Peace vs Justice*. Lanham: Rowman & Littlefield.

The Kerry Peace Initiative in the Israeli-Palestinian Conflict: When Hope and Good Intentions Are Not Enough

Amira Schiff
The Program on Conflict Management and Negotiation, Bar-Ilan University, Ramat Gan, 5290002, Israel
amira.schiff@biu.ac.il

Received 15 February 2016; accepted 7 February 2017

Abstract

This article examines the factors that contributed to the failure of the last major effort, which was carried out by US Secretary of State John Kerry, to facilitate a Final Status Agreement to resolve the Israeli-Palestinian conflict. The analysis is based on an understanding that every effort to resolve this intractable conflict, even if unsuccessful, is worthy of examination, which can yield interesting observations and insights that may inform future attempts to find a solution. As President Trump's administration makes intensive efforts to broker an Israeli-Palestinian peace agreement, and the US Middle East negotiation delegation shuttles intensively between the parties and between major regional actors to explore the possibility of renewing official negotiations, this seems like an opportune time to review the major factors that affected the outcome of the previous peace talks.

Keywords

John Kerry – Israeli-Palestinian conflict – ripeness theory – mutually enticing opportunities – central coalition theory

* Amira Schiff is on the faculty of the Conflict Resolution, Management and Negotiation program at Bar-Ilan University. Her research focuses on peace processes in ethno-political conflicts, such as the Israeli-Palestinian conflict, and in Sri-Lanka, Cyprus, Sudan and Aceh. She is the author of two books, *Readiness Theory and Peace Agreements in Intractable* Conflicts (2015) and *Conflict Resolution in the International Era* (forthcoming 2017).

 | DOI:10.1163/9789004393295_003

> We must continue the effort because it is in our national interest and because, despite many failures of the past, this conflict, like every conflict, must inevitably end.
>
> MITCHELL 2015: 339

Upon assuming office, US President Barack Obama was determined to bring the Israelis and Palestinians to the table to sign a Final Status Agreement and resolve their conflict. During Obama's terms in office, two major efforts were made to facilitate a Final Status Accord between the Israelis, led by Prime Minister Benjamin Netanyahu, and the Palestinians, led by Chairman Mahmoud Abbas.[1] The first took place in 2009–2010 under US Secretary of State Hillary Clinton and US Special Envoy for Middle East Peace George Mitchell. This dialogue started out as proximity talks that later developed into direct negotiations, following months of hard diplomacy. The initial hope was to resolve the Israeli-Palestinian conflict within one year. However, the direct negotiations reached a dead end very quickly. The second effort in 2013–2014, which produced longer direct negotiations between the parties, was mediated by US Secretary of State John Kerry, who was determined to succeed where his predecessor had failed. Yet, by the end of 2014, it was clear that Kerry's peace efforts had also failed.

The failure of this third-party mediation effort draws our attention to broader issues which are at the core of a classic debate in the conflict resolution field, and which pose an enigma to both scholars and to third parties considering engaging in intractable conflicts. The Kerry peace initiative was launched against the backdrop of unripe conflict. This structural condition tends to

---

1 In the 1993 Declaration of Principles (DOP) agreement, Israel and the Palestine Liberation Organization (PLO), acting on behalf of the Palestinians, committed to signing a final status agreement by the end of a five-year transition period. The Final Status Accord would resolve the core issues, bringing an end to the conflict and an end to the demands of both sides. In the framework of the Final Status Agreement, six core issues were to be resolved: the borders of the Palestinian state, Israel's security arrangements, the future status of Jerusalem, the refugee issue and the Palestinian demand for the right of return, the status of the Jewish settlements, and the allocation of water resources in the West Bank. To date, there have been three significant efforts to reach a final status agreement between Israel and the Palestinians with American mediation. The first occurred under President Clinton in 1999–2000, when Ehud Barak was Prime Minister of Israel and Yasser Arafat was President of the Palestinian Authority (PA). The second was the Annapolis process during the Bush administration in 2007–2008, during Ehud Olmert's tenure as prime minister and with Mahmoud Abbas serving as president of the PA. The third effort occurred in 2013–2014, between Prime Minister Benjamin Netanyahu and Chairman Mahmoud Abbas, with mediation by John Kerry, Secretary of State in the Obama administration.

reflect the prevailing situation in intractable conflicts, of which the Israeli-Palestinian conflict is a prime example, and raises the million dollar questions: Can a peace deal be struck under these conditions? Should a mediator attempt to mediate in a situation of unripe conflict? And what should a motivated third party do, or more precisely not do, in this situation in order to bring the parties to the negotiating table and reach an agreement? In the following analysis, I do not presume to have the answers to these questions, but rather provide an empirical study of the merits of the endeavor and their implications with respect to the consequences of yet another third-party attempt to resolve an intractable conflict.

The article applies the configurative case study methodology, applying concepts from three theories in the conflict resolution field to examine the factors that led to the failure of the efforts by Secretary of State Kerry, focusing on the factors that affected the outcome of the negotiation process. The first theory is ripeness theory, which outlines the necessary (albeit insufficient) conditions for the initiation of negotiation (Zartman 1999, 2000). We will also study the extent to which the mutually enticing opportunity (MEO) concept applies in our case. MEO is a rarely found alternative to the mutually hurting stalemate (MHS), which is central to the ripe moment concept. The second theory is the push and pull formulation, which is based on a revision and extension of ripeness theory elements into the negotiations phase in order to explain the results of negotiation. A main focus of this theory is the important role MEO plays in leading parties toward agreement (Zartman 2008; 2012). The third theory is central coalition theory (Pruitt 2005, 2007), which refers to the political dimension of readiness theory and allows us to study the internal political factors and coalition-building process affecting the result of the peace process.

The main argument in this article is that the failure of the process can be attributed to several elements, including factors relating to each party's preferences and internal politics, the parties' bilateral relations and the third party's conduct. This includes lack of ripeness, internal political pressures exerted on both leaders, gaps between the parties' positions and the Palestinians' perception of a valid unilateral track. Together with specific third-party conduct, these factors led to a negotiation process that failed to convince the parties that an agreement would be preferable to their unilateral choices. History presents many insights that can explain this failure and that go beyond the concepts we use in this article. Nonetheless, viewing the peace process through the prism of these three theories offers an interesting perspective that can contribute to understanding and simplifying the complex dynamics that led to yet another failure in this intractable conflict. Any attempt to resume the peace talks between the parties will have to take the factors presented in this article into consideration and find creative ways to address the types of problems Kerry encountered.

Background

At the outset of his first term, Obama set an ambitious goal of restarting Israeli-Palestinian peace talks. Obama was committed to resolving the Israeli-Palestinian conflict and believed in his ability to make the Israelis and Palestinians, in a rational way, resume negotiations, bridge their differences and resolve the conflict (Kirk, Wiser & Gilmore 2016).[2] His vision of the peace talks and agreement was very clear: a two-state solution, establishing a Palestinian state alongside Israel.

Signaling his commitment, during his first week in office, Obama appointed George Mitchell as his Special Envoy for Middle East Peace (Mitchell 2015: 317). This peace effort, which lasted until April 2011, was retrospectively described by Mitchell: "From the beginning to the end, it was an unsuccessful effort to bring together two leaders who share a deep, mutual mistrust" (Mitchell 2015: 338). Thus, this peace effort took place against the backdrop of heavy American pressure on both parties to renew negotiations.

Since 1991, US policy has been to encourage the parties to engage in direct negotiations. However, aware of the prevailing situation in the Israeli-Palestinian conflict in early 2009 and the difficulties Mitchell encountered in persuading the parties to resume negotiations, Obama first sought to create more favorable conditions for resumption of direct negotiations (Mitchell 2015: 325).[3] His administration tried hard to persuade the parties to make efforts to ease tensions. The Israelis, Palestinians and Arab states were all asked to make conciliatory gestures (Mitchell 2015: 325). The Palestinians were asked to prevent violence against Israel and reduce incitement in the Palestinian Authority (PA). Arab states were asked to take steps towards normalization with Israel,

2 Baker's interview in "Netanyahu at War," *Frontline*, January 5, 2016. Also note Obama's statement: "as history shows us that strong and sustained American engagement can bridge divides and build the capacity that supports progress." "Netanyahu at War" *Frontline*, January 5, 2016.

3 The difficult consequences of the fighting in Gaza between Israel and Hamas that began in late 2008 and continued through mid-January 2009 engendered intense hostility and tension between the Israelis and the Palestinians. In the wake of a criminal investigation launched against him, the prime minister of Israel Ehud Olmert resigned. Israel entered a heated election campaign, which led to the election of Netanyahu as prime minister (Mitchell 2015: 325).

and Israel was asked to freeze settlement construction (Mitchell 2015: 325). Obama viewed Israeli settlements as undermining the peace process and as an obstacle to peace.

For over a year, the US exerted tremendous efforts to help create an atmosphere in which meaningful negotiations could take place, but these efforts were unsuccessful. As Mitchell noted: "Attitudes hardened, and like the illusion of an oasis in the desert, the prospect of meaningful negotiation drifted further and further away from us" (Mitchell 2015: 326). It became clear that both sides were engaged in a public relations battle. "[They] contested every aspect of the process, always ... with a view toward the political effect at home" (Mitchell 2015: 331).

Upon assuming office in March 2009, Netanyahu called for direct negotiations and said he would not resume negotiations based on the discussions between Olmert and Abbas (Zanany 2015: 14–15; Diehl 2009).[4] Netanyahu initially refused to support the establishment of a Palestinian state. He insisted that any progress in negotiations be conditional upon Palestinian recognition of Israel as a Jewish state, and declared that Israel would not agree to a total freeze on settlement construction. The Arab states refused to make any gestures until Israel agreed to the freeze, and the Palestinians announced that anything less than a total freeze that included East Jerusalem would not be acceptable to them. From the Palestinians' perspective, it was all up to the Israelis (Mitchell 2015: 326).

Under heavy American pressure, Netanyahu endorsed the two-state solution for the first time in June 2009, calling for the establishment of a Palestinian state alongside the Jewish state (Kershner 2009). The US continued to pressure Netanyahu and in September, he agreed to a ten-month moratorium on new housing construction in settlements, set to begin in November 2009. Netanyahu called upon the Palestinians to respond by entering into direct negotiations. The Americans saw the moratorium as a very significant step. However, the Palestinians viewed it as "useless" and refused to start direct negotiations (Mitchell 2015: 329–330).

4 In the framework of the Annapolis peace process, a personal track between the leaders Olmert and Abbas, took place. These talks were intimate and based on mutual trust and understanding. In September 2008, Olmert presented Abbas with an "Agreement of Principles" that focused on the four core issues. Olmert's proposal was viewed favorably by the Palestinians, especially relative to previous proposals they had received from Israeli leaders (Zanany 2015: 14–15). Abbas did not reject Olmert's proposal, but also did not respond to it. In an interview Abbas gave in May 2009, he argued that the gaps between him and Olmert were wide. See Diehl (2009).

Months passed and the US realized in the spring of 2010 that it was futile to continue to push for direct negotiations. Instead, the Americans initiated proximity talks, with Mitchell meeting separately with each side to discuss all relevant issues. These talks "were to serve as a transition process that would lead to direct negotiations" (Mitchell 2015: 330). Through these talks, Mitchell's team hoped to gain a better understanding of the parties' positions in order to facilitate more meaningful discussions in direct negotiations in the future. At this point, the administration thought that negotiations, once begun, "should last no more than two years" (Rosen 2010).

The Israelis and the Palestinians approached the proximity talks differently, reflecting their deep mutual mistrust. As Mitchell noted, the talks "enabled them to gain a bit in the never-ending public relations battle" (Mitchell 2015: 330). The Palestinians accused the Israelis of publicly advocating direct negotiations while quietly erecting insurmountable barriers to any serious negotiation. The Israelis did not believe the Palestinians were willing to seriously negotiate. This was "a mirror image of the Palestinian belief that the Israelis were not serious about negotiations" (Mitchell 2015: 333).

By the summer of 2010, it was clear that the proximity talks were going nowhere. The moratorium, which reduced settlement construction, was slated to expire in late September. Netanyahu pushed hard to resume direct negotiations, confident that he could convince Abbas in a face-to-face meeting of his willingness to resolve the conflict. The Obama administration mobilized Jordan and Egypt to help pressure the Palestinians to agree to direct negotiations (Mitchell 2015: 334; Landler 2010). Abbas reluctantly agreed, conditioning his participation beyond September 2010 on an extension of the moratorium. The direct negotiations began on September 2, and the leaders met four times. During the direct talks, Hamas and Hezbollah threatened to sabotage the peace talks, and militant groups under Hamas began carrying out terror attacks against Israeli civilians.

As the talks between Netanyahu and Abbas commenced, immediate gaps emerged regarding the agenda, and the leaders' mutual distrust deepened. (Mitchell 2015: 334–336). The Palestinians threatened to leave the negotiations if the moratorium was not extended, while the Israelis rejected the US request to extend the settlement freeze. Netanyahu felt that Israel had not received the international credit it deserved for agreeing to the ten-month moratorium and had not gained any political benefit vis-à-vis the Palestinians. The Israelis were very annoyed that Abbas had waited until the ninth month of the moratorium to agree to direct negotiations (Mitchell 2015: 335). The Palestinians rejected Israel's offer to renew the moratorium in return for the recognition of Israel as a Jewish state. After four fruitless meetings, the direct negotiations ended (*Haaretz* 2010). Mitchell concluded: "Netanyahu does not believe that Abbas has the personal or political strength necessary to gain approval of an agreement with Israel. Abbas believed that Netanyahu is not sincere or serious about getting an agreement with the Palestinians and does only as much as he deems necessary to placate the United States. Since both men assume that negotiations will not succeed, neither has any incentive to take the political risks that will inevitably be required to make possible a peace agreement" (Mitchell 2015: 338).

During the years 2011–2012, several rounds of talks were held between senior Palestinians and Netanyahu and his emissaries. However, there was no breakthrough. Both sides were mainly engaged in blame games, trying to cast responsibility for the deadlock on the other side. In the wake of the deadlock, the Palestinians began taking unilateral steps. In September 2011, the Palestinians asked the United Nations (UN) Security Council to recognize the new State of Palestine, but were unable to mobilize the required majority. A year later, in November 2012, they turned to the UN again, this time to the General Assembly, requesting to upgrade their status in the organization to that of a non-member observer state. The Palestinian request was approved by a large majority.

Early in Obama's second term, the president appointed Secretary of State Kerry to oversee the Israel-Palestinian peace process. After intensive mediation engagement in an effort to revive negotiations, Kerry was able to formulate understandings for renewing the talks in July 2013.

Kerry set a very ambitious initial target for the talks: a comprehensive peace treaty for a two-state solution within about nine months. The Palestinians committed to enter into the talks and not to walk away from the negotiating table, and promised to freeze all unilateral steps against Israel in the UN during the nine-month period slated for negotiations (including the campaign of war crime allegations at the International Criminal Court [ICC]). The Palestinians demanded that Israel reciprocate with significant confidence-building measures: an indefinite freeze on construction over the 1967 "Green Line" and the release of 104 Palestinian prisoners imprisoned before the 1993 Oslo Accords. They also demanded that the talks be based on the 1967 lines as the international border. Israel agreed to a four-stage release of 104 Palestinian terrorists imprisoned for their involvement in murders of Israelis committed prior to the Oslo Accords and to significantly limit settlement construction during the months of negotiations (Birnbaum & Tibon 2014). The sides agreed in advance to discuss all of the core issues during the negotiations, and that the final accord would end the conflict and the demands of both sides.

In Israel, the agreement to release terrorists as a confidence-building measure was met with intense protests led by the families of the victims. The protests resumed at each stage of the prisoner release. Among Palestinians, there was criticism of the agreement to return to negotiations in the absence of a complete freeze on settlement construction as previously demanded (Birnbaum & Tibon 2014).

Based on the agreement to resume talks, Kerry sent a letter of guarantees to both sides, declaring that the US position was that the borders of the future Palestinian state should be based on the 1967 lines with land swaps (Birnbaum & Tibon 2014). At the same time, Kerry sent Israel a letter of guarantees clarifying that the US position was that the borders of the Palestinian state would not be identical to the 1967 lines; border adjustments would be made in accordance with the reality on the ground – implying recognition of the Sharon-Bush letter regarding the large settlement blocs. The letter of guarantees to Israel also made clear the US acceptance of the key demand that Israel be recognized as a Jewish state (Ravid 2013b).

Former US ambassador to Israel, Martin Indyk, was appointed to serve as special envoy for the peace process, responsible for facilitating the talks on behalf of the American administration. The US intended to play an active role in the talks: to oversee their progress, to resolve crises and to offer bridging proposals if necessary.

From the outset, there were wide gaps between the sides on all of the core issues, as well as considerable skepticism on both sides (Ravid 2013b; Birnbaum & Tibon 2014). The Israelis and Palestinians were unable to agree on the agenda for the talks. The Palestinians demanded that the negotiations begin by discussing borders and security arrangements, while Israel demanded that all of the core issues be discussed in parallel, fearing the talks might end after the borders were drawn, but without Palestinian concessions on refugee demands or other issues. Israel also insisted on reaching understandings on its demands for security arrangements before discussing the borders of the Palestinian state, and that, in any final agreement, Israel would maintain a military presence for decades in the West Bank, and along the Jordan River in particular. The Palestinians opposed any presence of Israeli soldiers or settlers in the territory in the framework of a final accord. On the subject of Jerusalem, the differences between the sides were even more profound. The Palestinians demanded a return to the situation that existed in the city prior to June 4, 1967, while the Israeli government rejected discussion of transferring sovereignty over parts of Jerusalem to the Palestinians.

On the key subject of refugees and historical responsibility, the Palestinians demanded that a number (to be determined by the two sides) of refugees and their descendants be allowed to return to Israel, as well as compensation for refugees and an Israeli declaration of responsibility. Israel refused to recognize any responsibility for 1948 refugees and rejected the Palestinian concept of a “right of return.”

In addition, in order to ensure the “end of conflict” and prevent future nationalist demands by Arab citizens of Israel, Israeli negotiators called for formal recognition of Israel as the nation-state of the Jewish people. The Palestinians countered that they had recognized Israel in the Oslo Accords and they refused to recognize Israel as a Jewish state for symbolic reasons pertaining to the Palestinian narrative vis-à-vis the conflict, and because they feared this would harm the rights of the Arab citizens of Israel (Ravid 2013b).

Under American leadership, Justice Minister Tzipi Livni and Yitzhak Molcho (Netanyahu’s representative) from the Israeli side, and Saeb Erekat and Mohammad Shtayyeh from the Palestinian side, met between August and December of 2013. These talks did not lead to a breakthrough. The two sides focused on presenting their basic positions, without the “give and take” expected in any negotiation (Birnbaum & Tibon 2014; Ravid 2014c). Following the second stage of the prisoner release, the Palestinian negotiating team resigned (again), alleging a massive wave of settlement construction.

Although Kerry had aimed to mediate direct talks between the two sides that would lead to a detailed final status accord, he realized by mid-November 2013 that, in light of the vast disagreement between the sides, this goal was unrealistic and that it would be better to focus on a framework agreement defining the borders of the two-state solution. At this stage, the Americans switched to indirect negotiations via proximity talks aimed at a more modest goal: the signing of a framework document by the end of March, outlining negotiations between the sides that would define the principles for resolving the core issues.

Kerry and Indyk conducted intensive contacts on the document, shuttled between the two sides and tried to bridge the gaps (Ravid 2014c). However, here too, after they reached some understandings with Netanyahu, the Americans discovered (in Kerry’s meeting with Abbas in Paris on February 19) that these terms were very far from what Abbas was ready to accept; the gaps between the sides were too wide, making it impossible to reach an agreement on this sort of framework document (Ravid 2014a; Ravid & Khoury 2014).

Kerry adopted an even more modest goal in late-February 2014: an American document of principles that both sides could accept, while expressing reservations about some of its content. The document of principles was designed to enable the continuation of the nine months of final status negotiations that were supposed to conclude in April 2014. The Americans understood that without reaching understandings on the document, it would be very difficult for Netanyahu to carry out the fourth and last round of prisoner releases, and that this would lead to the collapse of the entire process. Consequently, they began a marathon of conversations with the sides in order to extend the negotiations. However, the gaps between the sides were still too big (Birnbaum & Tibon 2014).

Under intense public pressure, Israel refused to release the fourth group of terrorists on the scheduled date unless the Palestinians promised not to quit the peace talks at the end of April, and committed to refrain from resuming unilateral action at the UN. Abbas, on his part, emphasized that if the prisoners were not released, he would not even consider extending the negotiations and would immediately resume unilateral action at the UN (Halevi 2014). The Palestinians rejected proposed alternatives to the prisoner release and refused to discuss the American compromise proposals for continuing the process; the Palestinians preferred to seek acceptance into international institutions, contrary to their commitments (Birnbaum & Tibon 2014; Yadlin 2014). A reconciliation agreement between the Palestine Liberation Organization (PLO), Hamas and Islamic Jihad on forming a unity government followed on April 23. Israel responded by suspending the talks.

In June 2014, tensions increased rapidly. Three Israeli teenagers were kidnapped and killed, followed by a revenge killing of a Palestinian boy and increased rocket fire from Hamas-controlled Gaza. This led to a seven-week war between Israel and Hamas. In October 2014, after this war ended, Kerry tried to promote a new diplomatic initiative as an alternative to the unilateral Palestinian efforts at the Security Council. Kerry checked with Netanyahu whether he would agree to an initiative that would include resuming negotiations on the borders of the Palestinian state, based on the 1967 lines with land swaps. Netanyahu did not reject Kerry's ideas out of hand (Khoury 2014). At the time, the Palestinians were trying to win the support of nine members of the Security Council for their request to define a timetable for ending the Israeli occupation of the West Bank in their quest to establish a state. The proposal was rejected by the Security Council in late December 2014 (Khoury 2014; Tibon 2014b). In early January 2015, the PA submitted a request to join 22 international conventions, including the Rome Statute of the ICC in The Hague.

Theory

Concepts taken from three theories may assist us in understanding the dynamics that led to the failure of the negotiations. The first is Zartman's ripeness theory. Ripeness is a crucial concept that is the first landmark on the path to successful achievement of outcomes in negotiation (Zartman 1999). This theory holds that a sense of ripeness is necessary for the productive inauguration of negotiations, whether bilateral or mediated (Zartman & deSoto 2010: 6). As Zartman argues: "A sense of ripeness may be required to turn negotiations for side effects … into negotiations to resolve conflict. In any case, unless the moment is ripe … the search for an agreed outcome cannot begin" (Zartman 2000: 227). The second theory is the attempt to revise and extend ripeness theory to the negotiation stage in the form of the "push and pull" model, which outlines two prerequisites for a positive outcome of negotiation: MHS as a push factor that impels the parties into negotiation, and MEO as a pull factor that "draws negotiation to a successful conclusion" (Zartman 2012: 304). The third theory is central coalition theory, which refers to the political dimension of readiness theory (Schiff 2014; Pruitt 2005: 8–15, 22; 2007: 1525, 1538).[5] This theory describes the internal political mechanism through which the parties decide to enter into negotiations and reach an agreement (Pruitt 2005, 2007).

Ripeness theory explains why and when parties to a conflict agree to negotiate, focusing on two necessary (albeit insufficient) conditions: MHS, optimally associated with an impending, past or recently avoided catastrophe, and a "way out" (WO) (Zartman 2000; Zartman & deSoto 2010). Both variables, MHS and WO, are perceptional and subjective, both are aided by objective evidence and both have to exist (though not necessarily at the same level) in both parties (Zartman 2008; Zartman & deSoto 2010).

> Mutually hurting stalemate occurs when the parties perceive that they are suffering in their current deadlock; they realize they cannot ignore

5 "Readiness" is a characteristic of a party in a conflict that reflects the thinking of the leadership regarding the conflict, and can vary within a wide range of conciliatory behavior (Pruitt 2005: 9–15; 2007: 1525). Readiness theory refers to a number of conditions that have the potential to bring parties to negotiation, and also provides an opportunity to examine various factors that influence the de-escalation of conflicts, including concession-making during negotiation (Schiff 2014). The theory describes the conditions appropriate for commencing negotiations in the language of psychological variables: motivation and optimism, each dependent on several variables. Motivation refers to the motivation to end the conflict and optimism is a sense that a mutually acceptable agreement is possible (Pruitt 2005: 8). Readiness theory is comprised of two parts (Pruitt 2007: 1538). The first part explains what will make the parties ready to de-escalate the conflict and relates to the parties as unitary actors. The second part, central coalition theory, relates to the internal politics of each side and examines the effect of political parties' level of readiness on achieving and implementing a peace agreement (Pruitt 2005: 22, 2007: 1538). Both parts of the theory can be used to explain the success or failure of peace processes (Pruitt 2007: 1538).

> the conflict and cannot escalate their way unilaterally to victory at an acceptable cost.
>
> ZARTMAN 2001: 4

> The idea behind the MHS concept is that, when the parties find themselves locked in a conflict from which they cannot escalate to victory and this deadlock is painful to both of them (although not necessarily in equal degrees or for the same reasons), they seek a way out.
>
> ZARTMAN 2000: 228

The second essential element – the perception of a WO – means that the parties must have a sense that it is possible to pursue an agreement in negotiation, and that the other side shares this sense and readiness to seek a solution. This perception of a WO in the context of an MHS gives the parties a sense that there is potential for progress (Zartman 2000: 228).

Still, scholars have indicated that there are also some rare cases in which parties might be pulled to agree to negotiate by the attraction of an MEO instead of being pushed to the table by a perception of a bad and worsening situation (Zartman 1999). One example of this was the Madrid Middle East peace process that began in 1991 under US mediation. This peace process was launched from a well-designed MEO, manipulated by a third party, who had to attract Israel and the PLO to engage in negotiations in the absence of MHS (Zartman 1999, 2000). Zartman (2000: 241) asserts that such ripe moments of MEO provide an opportunity for improvement in the situation "from a tiring rather than a painful deadlock." The enticement might be, for example, the prospect of winning at a lower cost than through conflict, or the potential for improved relations with a persistent mediator (Zartman 2000: 241). Yet, since there are very few cases of this phenomenon, the mechanisms of how MEOs entice the parties to start negotiations are still unclear. Still, as we will explain, an MEO is an important ingredient in the broader negotiation process and in enticing the parties to make the concessions necessary for reaching an agreement.

Zartman suggests that the components of ripeness theory, MHS and WO, may also help us understand the dynamics that lead to the successful conclusion of negotiation in an agreement. To prevent the parties from abandoning negotiation and pursuing a unilateral solution through escalation, the perception of ripeness must be maintained throughout the course of the negotiation itself. Thus, a perception of MHS serves as a factor that pushes the parties to begin negotiating. During the negotiation itself, this perception serves as a necessary but insufficient condition for success. For the parties to reach an agreement in the negotiation stage, the perception of MHS must be maintained, but the perception of WO must be transformed into a formula for solution that will create a perception of MEO. Consequently, MEO must develop in the negotiation and is a requisite condition for achieving agreement and resolving the conflict (Zartman 2008, 2012).

The MEO is created by the parties engaged in negotiation or by a third party (Zartman 2008, 2012). The parties must perceive the MEO as serving their needs and interests better than the status quo, and as offering hope for a change in the conflict. The challenge for negotiators and for a third party is to "put the elements into an attractive form with appropriate details" (Zartman 2012: 310), moving the negotiation from the formulation phase into the details phase and to agreement. During the negotiations, the terms of the resolving formula require adaptation, consistency and pressure to lead to a final accord (Zartman 2008). According to the theory, during the negotiation itself, the parties' procedural and substantive demands must be met in a resolving formula that will later become an MEO. The process must also be supported by external incentives and constraints to keep it on track.

A third party can play a major role in shaping the demands of the parties, adapting them to concessions that are acceptable to the other side. This mission requires maintaining a delicate balance between the demand and supply sides of the different antagonists in order to keep the parties negotiating. Thus, a third party can be of great help in formulating a resolving formula and convincing the parties to accept it, but the durability of the outcome will ultimately rest in the hands of the parties themselves (Zartman 2008: 238).

What will make a particular formula an enticing opportunity? The attractiveness of each formula is determined by the parties: they compare the value of the proposed solution to their needs and interests, and to their situation without an agreement or to the value of the status quo. Thus, the MEO can emerge when the parties are able to adapt their aims to correspond to achievable goals that will serve their interests and needs, and when they perceive the proposed agreement to offer greater benefits than continuing the conflict in an MHS or keeping the conflict unresolved in the form of a "soft stalemate" (Zartman 2008, 2012). Conversely, Zartman's studies stress that "negotiations fail when the parties – alone or with the help of a mediator – cannot find an MEO to pull themselves out of their conflict or noncooperation; that is, when they cannot find a formula for multi/bilateral solution to their situation that is preferable to unilateral solution or the status quo" (Zartman 2012: 304).

The third theory we refer to in our analysis is central coalition theory. This theory can explain why negotiations fail to produce the desired outcome and why, in some cases, the sides do reach an agreement (Pruitt 2007: 1531).

Central coalition theory relates to the readiness of the various factions on each side (and not just the leaders) to conduct negotiations with the other side in the conflict and reach an agreement. It describes the internal political mechanism through which the parties decide to enter into negotiations and reach an agreement (Pruitt 2005: 22–30; 2007: 1531–1534). It also describes the groups participating in peace negotiations as an alliance of doves from both sides and all of the groups that join them – that is, moderates and hawks (Pruitt 2007: 1538).

Pruitt argues that in the prenegotiation stage and during the course of negotiations, a "central coalition" sometimes coalesces that ranges from the hawks on each side of the conflict, to the moderates, to the doves, with the doves on each side adjacent to each other on this political spectrum (see Fig. 1). A central coalition can vary in size – from a very broad coalition that includes neutral factions, doves, moderates and most of the hawks, to a very narrow coalition that includes only the neutral factions and the doves (Pruitt 2005: 22; 2007: 1532–1533). As Pruitt (2005: 26) notes, when there is a large central coalition, "negotiation becomes quite likely; and if the coalition persists, a lasting agreement is likely to be reached."

On the political spectrum, the hawks have more extreme goals than the others, are more alienated from the other side and are more willing to take risks to achieve their objectives (Pruitt 2005: 22–23). They are often well-organized and well-armed, and this makes them a disproportionately powerful faction. There is a significant social distance between the hawks on the opposite sides of the conflict; they have different and contradictory values and narratives. On

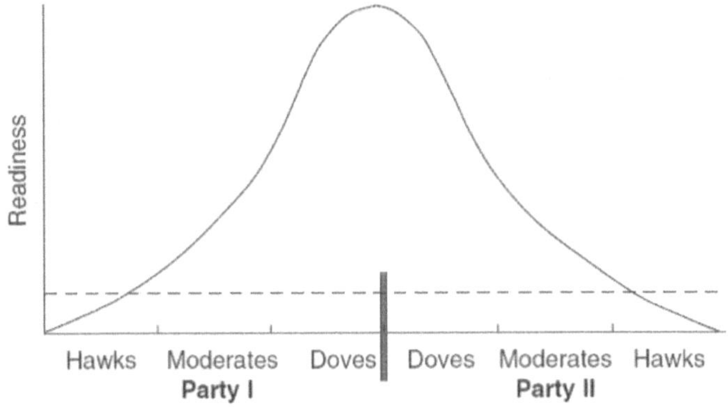

FIGURE 1 A sketch of a broad central coalition
SOURCE: PRUITT 2007: 1533

the other hand, the doves on both sides have similar views and can be in contact with each other in an effort to promote a peace process (Pruitt 2007: 1532).

According to this theory, all of the members of the central coalition must be above the threshold of readiness to advance toward an accord and accept it (Pruitt 2005: 26). The conflict will be ripe for resolution when there is a broad central coalition of people across the political spectrum who are ready to engage in negotiations (Pruitt 2007: 1532) (see Fig. 1). This theory contends: (a) the broader the central coalition (that is, the more groups on both sides that are above the threshold of readiness), the more successful the peace process will be; and (b) the central coalition must include most of the armed groups (Pruitt 2005: 22).

Readiness to negotiate will always be highest among doves and lowest among hawks, who will be less optimistic about the success of negotiations due to the extreme nature of their demands and their lack of trust in the other side. Therefore, they usually oppose negotiations and often act as "spoilers" to undermine an agreement if one is reached (Pruitt 2005: 24). Nonetheless, Pruitt maintains that hawks sometimes develop readiness for negotiating and become involved in talks that lead to an agreement when they find it acceptable. Political pressure from allies and moderate elements can also encourage extremists to opt for negotiations (Pruitt 2005: 24, 2007: 1533). The more well-organized and well-armed the extremists are on each side, the broader the coalition must be to neutralize the extremists and prevent them from undermining the negotiations and the agreement (Pruitt 2005: 25). A broad central coalition has a good chance of entering into negotiations and, if the readiness of the political factions increases, there will also be a greater chance of achieving an agreement that resolves the conflict. On the other hand, a narrow coalition might produce an agreement, but it will not be binding upon the rest of the group. Thus, it is unlikely to be a meaningful agreement.

Pruitt believes that leadership is a decisive component in forging a broad central coalition that is sustainable over time. If a political leader supports negotiations, the central coalition will be larger – especially if the leader is popular and is known as a patriot who can be counted on to protect the group's interests. A third party can also fill a role of similar importance in building a broad coalition (Pruitt 2005: 29–30).

The Kerry Peace Initiative: A Case Study of Failure

The failure of the Kerry peace initiatives can be attributed to different factors, including those relating to the parties and their relations, and to the third

party's conduct. The scope of this paper is too narrow to fully elaborate on all of them. Nonetheless, studying these mediation efforts in light of theories in the field (ripeness theory and its positive MEO alternative, the theory of the push and pull formulation, and central coalition theory) can help elucidate some of the major causes of this failure.

A Determined Third Party in an Unripe Conflict

Two factors underpin this negotiation process from its beginning to its end: a lack of ripeness and a determined third party. It was clear from the initial contacts to bring the parties to the table in 2013 that the conflict was not ripe for resolution. Yet Kerry, motivated by a sense of urgency, of a window of opportunity for reaching a two-state solution before it was too late, and hopeful that the leaders on both sides would be able to "find the way to compromise and to achieve both of their goals" (Kalman 2013), was determined to follow through with his initiative. Announcing the start of the peace negotiations, Kerry said:

> So while I understand the skepticism, I don't share it and I don't think we have time for it. I firmly believe the leaders ... can make peace for one simple reason: because they must. A viable two-state solution is the only way this conflict can end, and there is not much time to achieve it, and there is no other alternative. We all need to be strong in our belief in the possibility of peace.
>
> KERRY, LIVNI & EREKAT 2013

As we will explain, throughout the negotiation process, Kerry was aware of the parties' preferences and perceptions: Israel's preference to continue the status quo that was perceived as comfortable and the Palestinians preference to pursue the unilateral track. Kerry applied carrots and sticks in an effort to change the parties' perceptions of the conflict; he emphasized the potential opportunities in the event of a successful resolution of the conflict and the dangers inherent in the failure of the negotiations.

When the parties agreed to embark on negotiations, there was no perception of MHS and a WO. In the wake of Mitchell's failed peacemaking efforts, relations between the Palestinians and Israel were strained. These relations further deteriorated in May 2010, when Israel carried out the Gaza flotilla raid.[6]

6 In May 2010, a flotilla set sail from Turkey toward the Gaza Strip. According to the organizers, it was a humanitarian mission, intended to bring humanitarian supplies to the residents of the Gaza Strip, which had been blockaded since Hamas took control in June 2007. Six boats participated in the flotilla, carrying hundreds of pro-Palestinian passengers, members

Still, during Obama's first term and the beginning of his second term, there was no perception by the parties of a hurting impasse that was exacting an unbearable cost. Since 2011, the Palestinians have been conducting a campaign to win international recognition as a means of pressuring Israel's hardline government. The growing international criticism of Israel's ongoing settlement activity in the West Bank and the deadlocked negotiations contributed to the Palestinians' sense that time was on their side. Israel's right-wing government, which viewed the Palestinians as unwilling and unable to compromise, preferred the status quo. As noted, Israel also felt that the gestures Netanyahu had made in the previous round of dialogue were unappreciated. Prior to Kerry's efforts, both sides had posed preconditions for renewing negotiations and refused to comply with the other side's demands. The Palestinians insisted on the June 4, 1967 borders as the reference point for the negotiation on territory and demanded a total freeze on construction in the West Bank and in East Jerusalem. Israel's preconditions included a demand that the Palestinians recognize Israel as a Jewish state (Dekel, Kurtz & Sher 2014).

There was also no perception of a WO. In light of the unsuccessful dialogue conducted during Obama's first term, the lack of trust between the leaders was profound, the gaps between the sides on all of the core issues were wide and there was great skepticism on both sides about the other's willingness to reach an agreement acceptable to both parties (Cohen 2013; Ravid 2013b). The Palestinians believed that Israel was not interested in ending its control of Palestinian territory and halting settlement activity in the West Bank. In the Palestinian view, the Israeli government had agreed to negotiate in order to ease international pressure and would exploit the talks to blame the Palestinians for the deadlock in the peace process. Israel, on the other hand,

---

of Islamic organizations (including IHH Humanitarian Relief Foundation," one of the organizers of the flotilla), politicians and a number of journalists. They were also joined by about 40 mercenaries with the aim of creating a violent confrontation. Israel offered the organizers of the flotilla to deliver the humanitarian supplies via the Israeli and Egyptian border crossings after inspections by UN and Red Cross officials. The flotilla participants rejected this proposal and continued to sail toward the Gaza Strip. In Israel's view, the flotilla's true objective was to support Hamas terrorism by creating a provocation designed to challenge Israel's right to fight terror. As the flotilla continued toward the Gaza Strip, Israeli fighters boarded and commandeered the ship outside of Israel's territorial waters. During the takeover of the largest ship, *Mavi Marmara,* there was a violent confrontation. Armed passengers seized some of the Israel Defense Forces (IDF) soldiers, injuring ten of them. Nine passengers were killed and 20 injured; most were associated with the IHH organization or other Turkish Islamic organizations. The incident stirred a media frenzy in Israel and in the world, and relations between Israel and Turkey were severely strained.

thought the Palestinians were unwilling to accept the solution of two states for two peoples, did not recognize Israel's right to exist, and basically sought to annihilate Israel in the long run (Brom, Dekel & Kurtz 2015). Thus, embarking on the 2013 negotiations, the leaders' assessment of the likelihood of reaching a final accord within nine months, as Kerry expected, was very low.

Kerry had to operate in these complicated circumstances. Motivated by the US interest in resolving the Israeli-Palestinian conflict during this period of instability in the Middle East, and led by his strong belief that the parties had only one or two years before running out of time to achieve a two-state solution, Kerry pressed both leaders to agree to negotiate and tried to change the parties' perceptions of threats and opportunities (Sherwood 2013). Aaron David Miller, a former Middle East peace negotiator and adviser to several US administrations, noted that the negotiations "would not have occurred without John Kerry" (Lakshmanan & Gaouette 2013).

The US believed that in light of the growing instability in the Middle East, it was an opportune time to boost stability in the region by resolving the Israeli-Palestinian conflict, which involves the most moderate parties in the region.[7] As Miller explains, Kerry believed "that Israeli-Palestinian peace is an important US interest," and that "compared with the risk-to-reward ratio of intervening in Syria, the Israeli-Palestinian conflict offers a safer, and perhaps smarter, bet. Indeed, it's the one issue in the region where US interests and values coincide with something else: the possibility that US diplomacy might actually make a difference" (Miller 2013). Kerry himself held strongly to the belief that the status quo in the protracted Israeli-Palestinian conflict was not sustainable and not static, and that "a viable two-state solution is the only way this conflict can end, and there is not much time to achieve it, and there is no alternative" (Kerry, Livni & Erekat 2013b). As he saw it, the months he spent shuttling back and forth between the leaders, trying to convince them to renew negotiation, were critical for Israel and for Palestinians. The results of his mission, he believed, would dictate the nature of Israeli-Palestinian relations in the coming decades. Kerry believed there would be no other chance to resolve the conflict (Kalman 2013). Aware of the parties' comfort with the status quo, Kerry had to produce some incentives to motivate them to embark on negotiation (Kalman 2013; Kerry 2013; Kerry, Livni & Erekat 2013). This included cultivating perceptions of looming catastrophe and of the rewards of a future without conflict. Thus, he stressed that failure to resolve the conflict at this juncture would result in serious short-term and long-term consequences for both parties, including the threat of renewed intifada against Israel, the collapse of the PA, the rise

7 See Vice President Joe Biden's keynote address at J Street's 2013 national conference.

of extremist Islam in the West Bank, an intensified delegitimization campaign against Israel, renewed Palestinian efforts to join international organizations, and Israel would need to choose to be either Jewish or democratic. On the other hand, he also stressed the far-reaching benefits – economic, security and stability – that would be in everyone's interest if the conflict was to be resolved (Kerry 2013). Beyond describing the opportunities entailed in agreement, and in an effort to pull the parties to the table, Kerry offered the PA an economic investment package of $4 billion, and offered Israel help from US Marine General John Allen in appraising what security measures it would need to ensure its safety under a two-state solution (Lakshmanan & Gaouette 2013). Both sides were susceptible to massive American and international pressure to agree to negotiate and accept Kerry's terms (Birnbaum & Tibon 2014; Cohen 2013). Both leaders were worried about the consequences if Kerry's efforts to resume negotiations collapsed (Miller 2013). The Palestinians feared the diplomatic and economic cost they would bear and Israel feared the diplomatic cost. Both leaders, Netanyahu and Abbas, were also worried about being blamed personally if Kerry's efforts to resume negotiations failed (Miller 2013). Abbas was concerned that a refusal to renew talks would lead to a cutoff of aid to the Palestinians and the imposition of sanctions by the US and Israel, which might lead to a collapse of the PA (Cohen 2013). Israel, on its part, realized its interests in complying with Kerry's efforts to renew the peace process, even if it was skeptical at the chances of its success. Rejecting the US peace initiative could trigger European threats of boycotts and sanctions. Israel also saw importance in preserving the momentum of dialogue in order to restrain the Palestinians from turning to violence or pursuing additional unilateral action in the UN. From Israel's perspective, the negotiations offered a possible opportunity to reach an agreement that would block the formation of a binational state, maintain Israel's Jewish identity and prevent the creation of another Iranian proxy terrorist state on Israel's border (Lakshmanan & Gaouette 2013). Thus, despite their skepticism regarding the chances of reaching an agreement, both leaders, Netanyahu and Abbas, were dragged into the talks because of the need to maintain good relations with the US and the international community, and to avoid paying the cost of rejecting the US peace efforts.

Still, Kerry's efforts to portray the looming threats and to offer attractive peace dividends were not enough to outweigh the distrust between the sides, which grew even more acute during the negotiations (Birnbaum & Tibon 2014). As we will explain, internal political pressures exerted on the leaders of both sides, as well as some key elements in the parties' conduct, made it more difficult to generate public support for an agreement on both sides. All of these factors, in addition to the ineffective way in which the Americans mediated, limited the possibility that the 2013–2014 negotiations would actually produce a sense in the parties that a resolving formula was taking form (Brom 2014; Yadlin 2014).

Despite the lack of meaningful progress in the negotiation, the US pressed to continue the talks, in part to prevent escalation in the West Bank. Kerry also rallied the donor states, led by the US, to put together an additional assistance package for the Palestinians (Harel 2013). However, none of this helped to change the parties' approach. After nine months of negotiations, Abbas was accusing Netanyahu of refusing to recognize a Palestinian state in the 1967 borders, and he viewed Netanyahu's insistence on recognizing Israel as a Jewish state as proof of the prime minister's unwillingness to make peace. On Israel's part, what eventually struck a final, destructive chord vis-à-vis negotiations was the reconciliation pact between Fatah and Hamas in late April 2014 and Fatah's agreement to form a unity government with Hamas – despite Hamas' declarations that it would not recognize Israel or abandon the path of terrorism (Birnbaum & Tibon 2014; Yadlin 2014).

The Third Party's Conduct

Three key elements in the American mediation effort were unconducive to the emergence of MEO perceptions during the negotiation and ultimately contributed to the failure of the process: setting a goal that was too ambitious and unrealistic; the appearance and perhaps the substance of asymmetrical conduct; and a lack of understanding of the complex political and cultural factors on both sides. The complex political circumstances will be discussed in the next section.

First, Kerry's initial goal of reaching a final agreement within nine months was clearly too ambitious and disconnected from the political context and realities in a region that has known many failures. In light of the parties' failure to recognize during the prenegotiation stage that they were trapped in a costly predicament and had no unilateral alternatives for winning the conflict, the lack of mutual trust that only deepened during the negotiation, and the internal political limitations of each, it is hard to understand how Kerry ever thought he could resolve the conflict, especially in such a limited period of time. The American mediator was apparently the only one who harbored any expectations of success – expectations that were not shared by either the Palestinian side or the Israeli side (Birnbaum & Tibon 2014).

The failure to generate a formula perceived as attractive by the parties during the negotiation can also be attributed to the mediator's conduct in the complex environment of asymmetric conflict. Asymmetry is "a subjective notion that is based on the parties' perceived understanding of the asymmetrical relationship" (Aggestam 2002: 87). Therefore, it is "significant that the mediators understand and take into account the parties' perceptions of asymmetry" (Aggestam 2002: 74). Yet it appears that the Kerry team failed to do this in its asymmetrical conduct, as perceived by the two sides. The Americans saw the Palestinians as the weaker party, and their own position was often closer to that of the Palestinians, particularly on settlements (Ravid 2014c). They also assumed that Abbas was already prepared to make far-reaching concessions (Birnbaum & Tibon 2014). Consequently, the US team invested most of its efforts vis-à-vis Netanyahu and Israel. Fearing that the Palestinians would lock into a recalcitrant position, the Americans decided not to present any proposal to them until they felt that the contacts with Israel were significantly productive. The result was marathon conversations focused on the Israeli side, including intensive discussions with Israel on the framework document – both with Minister Tzipi Livni, who led the effort to formulate the document, and through negotiations conducted directly between Netanyahu and Kerry in videoconferences held almost daily. Kerry exerted heavy pressure on Israel to accept the framework agreement; he refrained from investing similar efforts vis-à-vis Abbas (Ravid 2014c). For example, in an effort to influence public opinion in Israel as the negotiations faltered in November 2013, the Secretary of State said: "The alternative to getting back to the talks is the potential of chaos. I mean does Israel want a third intifada? ... I believe that if we do not resolve the issues between Palestinians and Israelis ... there will be an increasing isolation of Israel, there will be an increasing campaign of de-legitimization of Israel ... If we don't end the presence of Israeli soldiers perpetually within the West Bank, then there will be an increasing feeling that if you cannot get peace with a leadership that is committed to non-violence, you may wind up with leadership that is committed to violence" (ICRS 2013). On another occasion, he made an exceptional public statement on the alleged danger Israel faced from boycotts and international isolation if it failed to reach an accord, arguing that Israel would become an apartheid state if it did not achieve peace (Ravid 2014b). This received extensive publicity in Israel, much of it highly critical (Yaar & Hermann 2014b; Ravid 2014b). The American pressure exerted on the Netanyahu government to moderate its stance was perceived by the Israeli public as unfair and as a misguided effort aimed at pushing Israel toward unacceptable concessions (Yaar & Hermann 2014b).

Meanwhile, as Kerry invested time and effort in convincing Israel to accept the framework agreement, and paid less attention to the Palestinians, the Palestinians felt slighted which contributed to them adhering strongly to their stance. Furthermore, understanding that Israel, pressured by the US, would have to pay a heavy price if it refused to compromise on the core issues, the

Palestinians felt encouraged to adopt a rigid stance (Yadlin 2014). Thus, the asymmetry in mediation contributed to a hardening of the Palestinian position, as reflected in Abbas' refusal to discuss the American document of principles and compromise proposals for extending the process.

As noted, the Americans did not want to present the Palestinians with an insignificant proposal, fearing that this might diminish the Palestinians' willingness to cooperate. Thus, the Americans refrained from discussing with the Palestinians the document it formulated with Netanyahu until the document was already in an advanced stage (Ravid 2014c). However, the mediator's conduct led to precisely the situation the Americans feared. When Kerry met Abbas in Paris on February 19, 2014 and presented to him orally the key points of the document he had formulated with Netanyahu, Abbas – who thought that Kerry was trying to sell him a finished product – refused to conduct talks on the framework document and insisted that Israel first release all of the prisoners included in the commitment ostensibly made at the beginning of the negotiations. In efforts to negotiate with Abbas a month later, including the meeting with Obama in mid-March 2014, the Palestinian president continued to refuse to discuss the framework agreement, which he saw as a conspiracy against him. He only agreed to give Obama a vague promise that he would get back to Obama within a few days with a response regarding the framework document. But this never happened (Ravid 2014a; Friedman 2014).

American and Israeli officials involved in the talks on the framework document noted that, during the negotiations and work on the document, Netanyahu indeed slowly but consistently softened his views, and showed seriousness and readiness to move forward (Friedman 2014; Birnbaum & Tibon 2014). Martin Indyk is quoted as saying that after six months of direct negotiations between the parties, Netanyahu moved into the "zone of a possible agreement" and was prepared to make substantial concessions (Friedman 2014). Yet, the Palestinians perceived the American proposals as reflecting the Israeli position on all of the important issues (Khalidi 2014). As drafts of the document of principles went back and forth between Washington and Jerusalem on a daily basis, the wariness of the Palestinians and their frustration with the Americans became even deeper; ultimately, the Palestinians lost interest in the process (Birnbaum & Tibon 2014). As in similar identity-based conflicts, it appears that the lack of trust between the parties heightened fears and made a reactive devaluation of an agreement more likely.

According to Zartman (2008: 232, 234), the attractiveness of each proposed formula in negotiations is determined by the parties: they compare the value of the proposed solution to their needs and interests, and to their situation without an agreement or to the value of the status quo. For many years, the

Palestinians believed that international institutions such as the ICC would serve as a powerful instrument for exerting international pressure on Israel. Consequently, during the negotiations, the Palestinians still perceived the unilateral track as preferable to the status quo, thus undermining the development of MEO (Rudoren 2014).[8] The negotiation framework defined in advance by the US enabled the Palestinians to choose the unilateral path at the end of the nine months of negotiations, without exacting a cost for their refusal to consider or respond to proposed compromise formulas. The US refrained from applying its leverage of "limitation" – that is, its "ability to close off parties' alternatives for winning ... the conflict" (Touval & Zartman 2001: 437).

The Palestinians justified their decision to pursue the unilateral path (applying for acceptance into international institutions and submitting a proposal to the Security Council to end the conflict) as a response to the delay in carrying out the fourth round of the prisoner release and the announcement of Israeli construction. However, it appears that already in October 2013, the Palestinians began drafting a "Plan B" that included resuming a UN campaign, and were threatening to quit negotiations already during the talks that took place in November 2013 (Birnbaum & Tibon 2014; Halevi 2014). In March 2014, the Palestinians refused to discuss the American compromise proposals for continuing the process, though still within the framework of their nine-month commitment (Halevi 2014).[9] They preferred to seek acceptance into international institutions, contrary to their commitment (Birnbaum & Tibon 2014). It appears that the Palestinian leadership determined that the cost of saying "yes" to the American proposal to continue the negotiations was higher than the cost of turning to the unilateral path.

The Parties' Internal Politics

Another way of explaining why the negotiations failed to produce the desired outcome is through political analysis based on central coalition theory (Pruitt 2005, 2007). According to this theory, all of the members of the "central

8 This step was expected to be welcomed by the Palestinian public and to boost the standing of the PA and its leader, Abbas, whose popularity dropped after the conflict in Gaza. In a survey conducted by the Palestinian Center for Policy and Research, 80% of the respondents supported joining additional international bodies, and 75% supported joining the ICC. See Rudoren (2014).

9 In March 2014, Saeb Erekat, a member of the PLO executive committee and head of the Palestinian negotiating team, reportedly prepared a 65-page document that surveyed the developments in the diplomatic process and offered a list of recommendations for the PA, some of which Abbas implemented in early April. See Halevi (2014).

coalition" must be above the threshold of readiness – that is, have the requisite motivation and optimism to advance toward an accord and accept it (Pruitt 2005: 26). The Israeli-Palestinian process was characterized by a very narrow central coalition, driven by the leaders on both sides, Netanyahu and Abbas, who understood the importance of complying with the American efforts to start negotiation. They managed to overcome and manipulate internal political constraints to come to the negotiating table, but subsequent processes allowed the hawks to set the tone and sow pessimism vis-à-vis the negotiations.

From the outset, the political atmosphere on both the Israeli and Palestinian sides did not encourage progress in the peace process Kerry initiated. On the Palestinian side, Abbas was weak within his own political camp and lacked legitimacy among the Palestinian public at large (Cohen 2013). Prior to Kerry's announcement about resuming negotiations, the PLO's Executive Committee voted against participating in negotiations with Israel in light of Israel's rejection of the Palestinians' preconditions (a commitment to the 1967 borders and a settlement freeze). Nonetheless, Abbas decided to renew the negotiations and was heavily criticized for this step. Furthermore, elections were long overdue and internal conflict unrelated to Israel was increasing (Brom 2014). Palestinian society was immersed in a deep political crisis, with a rift between the West Bank, ruled by Fatah, and the Gaza Strip, ruled by Hamas, which fiercely opposed Abbas' diplomatic efforts. In Abbas' own Fatah party, there were also reservations about negotiating with the Netanyahu government, which was a fragmented coalition perceived by the Palestinians as unlikely to make or sustain major concessions (Birnbaum & Tibon 2014; Rabbani 2014; Cohen 2013). Abbas was accused by members of the PLO Executive Committee of acting like a dictator, disregarding the decisions of PLO institutions and withdrawing his own demand for a total freeze in settlement construction (Cohen 2013).

Eventually, American pressure tipped the scales in favor of the negotiation process, but the pessimistic mood in internal Palestinian politics did not change throughout the months of the negotiations. Abbas and various prominent PLO figures accused Israel of placing obstacles in the negotiations and of not being sincerely interested in peacemaking (Cohen 2013). Pessimism grew stronger and many senior Palestinian figures favored returning to unilateral action at the UN and applying international pressure on Israel (Birnbaum & Tibon 2014; Halevi 2014).

Netanyahu's government was a fragile coalition that was liable to collapse if major concessions were made without the expected quid pro quo, particularly on the refugee claims. Most of the Knesset members in Netanyahu's hardline Likud party and coalition partners (including Yisrael Beiteinu and

Jewish Home) were skeptical regarding the claim that the establishment of a Palestinian state would bring peace (Tzena 2013; Cohen 2013; Brom 2014). Based on the dialogue conducted during Mitchell's term, Netanyahu felt that the risks he took in endorsing the two-state solution and the ten-month settlement moratorium were not appreciated and reciprocated (Birnbaum & Tibon 2014). Thus, from the outset of Kerry's dialogue with Netanyahu about Palestinian demands for a settlement freeze and the release of 104 prisoners, Netanyahu was sure his right-wing party, the Likud, would never accept it. Neither would the more hardline Jewish Home party, his coalition partner. It wasn't even certain that the coalitions' two centrist parties would (Birnbaum & Tibon 2014). Nonetheless, in the face of European threats of boycotts and sanctions, and after consulting with his coalition partners, Netanyahu agreed to renew negotiations. As part of this agreement, Kerry consented to modify some of the conditions: the prisoners would be released in four rounds over the nine months of talks, and the freeze would not be total – some new settlement units would be approved (Birnbaum & Tibon 2014).

Central coalition theory also turns our attention to the role of the leadership in forging a broad coalition, as Pruitt (2005: 29–30) observes. Both leaders, Netanyahu and Abbas, understood the importance of complying with the US request to restart the peace process and devised ways to overcome political constraints and expand their central coalition. Netanyahu, realizing the release of 104 Palestinian prisoners would be a bitter pill for his right-wing coalition partners to swallow, came up with a compromise formula: some settlement construction in exchange for the release of prisoners in four stages. Fearing he lacked a government majority on the prisoner release deal, Netanyahu withheld information from most of the government ministers, who first saw the text of the decision when it came up for a vote, leaving many of them unsure of what they were voting on. At the same time, Netanyahu released a letter to the Israeli public, explaining the reasons for the prisoner release and stressing its importance for the State of Israel. Netanyahu noted that prime ministers must sometimes make tough decisions that run contrary to public opinion and he acknowledged the pain this particular decision caused to bereaved Israeli families. It was especially important to examine the possibility of resolving the conflict with the Palestinians at this time, he explained, in light of the changes in the Middle East (Ravid & Khoury 2013; Segal 2013b).

When a crisis arose prior to the fourth round of the prisoner release, Kerry tried to cobble together a deal to prevent the talks from collapsing, and the Palestinians from resuming their UN bid. Under Kerry's proposal, Israel would release the fourth group of prisoners, free another 400 prisoners of its own choosing and halt all new settlement announcements in the West Bank, excluding Jerusalem (that is, a partial freeze) (Birnbaum & Tibon 2014; Landler & Gordon 2014). In return, the Palestinians would be obliged to continue negotiating for another nine months and Netanyahu would win the release of Jonathan Pollard, a convicted Jewish-American spy whose release Israeli prime ministers had sought for decades. Netanyahu was ready to accept the proposal and Abbas also signaled his willingness (Birnbaum & Tibon 2014). The April 1 deadline the Palestinians had set for the prisoner release was fast approaching and Kerry promised the Palestinians that Israel would promptly vote on the latest proposal (Birnbaum & Tibon 2014). However, as the Pollard deal was still being finalized and Netanyahu was lobbying his coalition partners, Abbas was being urged by hawkish figures like Saeb Erekat (the chief Palestinian negotiator) not to wait any longer to sign fifteen UN conventions, which he indeed went ahead and signed (Birnbaum & Tibon 2014).

Abbas was also under heavy American pressure to enter into negotiations. Yet he and others in the PLO doubted Netanyahu's intentions and were skeptical of the chances of success. "If the Palestinians were going to enter futile talks, they should get something tangible to show for it," he insisted (Birnbaum & Tibon 2014). The Palestinians were ready to suspend their campaign for UN recognition and renew negotiations in exchange for the release of the 104 pre-Oslo prisoners. Abbas could then fend off internal critics by contending that his consent to renew negotiations with Israel won the release of the prisoners. The Palestinian leadership also stressed that the suspension of the campaign in the UN was limited to the nine-month period of negotiations, and if Israel would not agree to a two-state solution along the lines of the 1967 borders, many additional states would recognize Palestine as a UN member-state and condemn settlement construction as illegal, including in Jerusalem (Cohen 2013). Prior to beginning negotiations, Abbas also demanded a letter from Kerry affirming that the US position was that the Israeli-Palestinian borders should be based on the 1967 lines with mutually agreed land swaps. Ultimately, as noted, when the crisis erupted in March 2014 over the fourth round of the prisoner release, Erekat, who had been urging Abbas for months to quit the talks, convinced Abbas not to wait any longer for Israel's decision and to proceed with the Palestinians' UN initiatives (Birnbaum & Tibon 2014).

Further Erosion of Trust Between the Parties

The prisoner release and settlement freeze were intended as confidence-building measures, yet they proved counterproductive, further undermining trust, eroding the internal political support within each camp and allowing the hawks to set the tone. From Israel's perspective, the deal was for the release of prisoners in exchange for construction in the settlements. That is, the release of terrorists meant that talks would resume without a total freeze on building new housing units in the settlements, only a slowdown in construction (Ravid 2013a; Ravid & Khoury 2013). Netanyahu requested Kerry's consent for construction of over 2,000 new settlement units in order to win his coalition's support for the prisoner release. In Netanyahu's mind, his agreement to a partial freeze did not include long-term building plans or East Jerusalem, which Israel considered sovereign territory (Birnbaum & Tibon 2014; Segal 2013). Kerry was said to be focusing on the big picture of steering a process that would finally resolve the Israeli-Palestinian conflict. He hurried to announce the resumption of talks, without asking for clarifications. Here, at least, what was intended to strengthen Abbas actually ended up weakening him politically. The Palestinians, who were willing to suspend their UN recognition campaign in return for a total freeze in settlements, were furious about the approval of even moderate construction. Members of the PLO Executive Committee argued against resuming negotiations, claiming that Israel's systematic actions were destroying any chance of a two-state solution and undermining international efforts to implement the principle of two states demarcated by the 1967 borders (Cohen 2013).

On the other hand, the Palestinians failed to understand that the release of murderers is a very sensitive issue in Israeli society. The celebrations in the Palestinian street for the released prisoners convicted of murdering Israelis had a very strong negative impact on public opinion in Israel (Channel 2 News 2013). Thousands of Israelis gathered to protest the prime minister's decision to release terrorists. Netanyahu's coalition partners from the Jewish Home and Yisrael Beiteinu parties also opposed the release of Palestinian prisoners and had tried to pass a legislative measure to block the second round of the prisoner release. Their legislative proposal fell in the Ministerial Committee on Legislation after the prime minister put heavy pressure on the ministers to reject the bill (Cohen & Khoury 2013; Liss 2013).

Incitement was also a major issue that undermined any chance of building trust between the parties during the negotiation process. Israelis were very sensitive to what they viewed as incitement in the PA by officials close to Abbas, as well as in the education system and Palestinian media – incitement against the existence of Israel, of denying the Jews' connection to the Holy Land, of preaching that Israel would inevitably and soon disappear, of portraying the Jews as subhuman creatures who should be treated as such, and of declaring that all forms of resistance, including terrorism, are legitimate for achieving the final goal. The ongoing incitement since the signing of the Declaration of Principles in 1993 undermined the legitimacy of the peace accord among the

Palestinian public, and eroded Israelis' belief in the possibility of achieving a stable peace based on two states (Yaar & Hermann 2014a).

Conclusions

In this article, we tried to identify factors that contributed to the failure of the Kerry peace initiative, including factors related to the parties, their relations and to the third party. We explained how Kerry, a motivated mediator, had to find ways of convincing the parties that negotiation was preferable to other options, and pressured them to exploit the opportunity to negotiate and make mutual concessions in pursuit of an agreement.

Third parties who try to mediate in intractable conflicts like the Israeli-Palestinian conflict face a difficult and complicated challenge. In these conflicts, peace initiatives more often fail than succeed. These peace initiatives usually take place in the context of unripe conflicts, and mediators, driven by their interests and beliefs, must devise ways to bring the parties to the negotiation table – and if they succeed in this task, the mediators must then prod the parties toward an agreement.

Third parties have a major role to play in mediating conflicts, whether ripe or unripe for resolution. In conflicts that are ripe, a third party can play a facilitating role in launching the negotiations; when conditions are not ripe, it can help in "ripening the conflict objectively and in changing the parties' perception of it" (Zartman & deSoto 2010: 8). Alternatively, as Secretary of State James Baker exemplified in the process leading to the Madrid conference in October 1991, a third party can play a major role as a manipulative mediator, creating an MEO to convince the parties to negotiate. Once the negotiations begin, the mediator can be of invaluable assistance in keeping the parties in the negotiation track, in orchestrating a resolving formula and in encouraging the parties to see its attractiveness. The mediator certainly faces formidable challenges in these cases. In intractable conflicts where the parties are locked into the conflict dynamics and prefer the status quo or unilateral track, these challenges sometimes seem insurmountable.

Expressing his hopefulness in the leaders' ability to "heed the call of history" (Kerry, Livni & Erekat 2013), Kerry decided to act in a situation in which conditions were not ripe for resolving the conflict: the parties did not feel trapped in an uncomfortable and costly predicament, and believed they had satisfactory unilateral alternatives to negotiation. Believing he could change the parties' perceptions about the pros and cons of resolving their conflict at that point in time, Kerry worked hard to create a sense of urgency of a looming catastrophe for both parties if they failed to resolve their conflict during this window of opportunity. In addition, both parties were led to believe that their refusal to negotiate would incur costs and hurt their relationship with the United States. The mediator also proposed a deal that both leaders could use to prop up internal support for their change in policy when agreeing to negotiate. Still, the parties did not believe there was someone to talk with on the other side or something to talk about. In this respect, the Kerry peace process can be viewed as another example of parties that were pulled to the table by an MEO, in which the "relations with the mediator may be the key to the improved situation, occasioning a mediator's role as manipulator" (Zartman 1999: 6). Again, we see that this is not a sufficient condition for the parties to reach an agreement in an intractable conflict when the parties do not perceive themselves to be in a painful impasse. As Miller (2013) pointed out, Kerry might have gotten the parties to the negotiating table, but he could not keep them there, let alone reach an agreement. The basic and entrenched mistrust between the parties, which actually moved them further apart during the talks, the internal political pressures exerted on both leaders (reflecting a narrow central coalition), the gaps between the parties' positions, the Palestinians' perception of a valid unilateral track, and the specific conduct of the third party, which served to increase the skepticism and mistrust by the parties, all combined to prevent the negotiation process from generating a perception of a promising resolving formula.

Bercovitch (2009: 349) argues that a number of factors affect the choice of a mediation strategy and its potential for success. Among the most important factors, he lists "the previous relationship and experience of the parties." He notes: "any current conflict management is affected by previous conflict management efforts and any learning which may have taken place … Mediators may use information from previous efforts, or build on any rapport they may have had with the parties." Still, it appears that the lessons from the failure of the Mitchell shuttle diplomacy were not learned. By setting the ambitious goal of resolving the Israeli-Palestinian conflict despite the lack of ripe conditions on the ground, and by what was perceived by both sides as asymmetrical conduct during the negotiations, Kerry's mediation seems to have only deepened the mistrust and underlined the gaps between the parties. In this light, Miller's words (2016) are particularly insightful and thought provoking: "As the fix-it people, Americans have a hard time accepting that we can't sort out conflicts when those directly involved aren't willing or able to do so. But sometimes, it makes more sense for our diplomats and negotiators to stay home rather than look weak and ineffective while searching for solutions to problems they simply cannot resolve." This also leads us to one major lesson of the failure of the Kerry peace initiative: that the goal of a third party in the future must be more modest. Any future effort must be based on an understanding of the need to return to a calculated format of a gradual and constructive process of conflict management, while creating a political horizon that is sufficiently attractive to both sides in terms of their interests. In any future efforts, the mediator should carefully plan his moves, gauge his ability to maneuver and weigh his options in light of the internal political constraints and the way each side calculates costs and benefits. As President Trump's administration attempts to create conditions for a broader regional peace deal among Israel, Palestinian and Arab states, a grand regional approach appears to be taking shape. Since this approach takes into account shared regional interests, and enlarges the pie for both Israel and the Palestinians, it just might be the first step in this direction.

Chronology of Events

January 2009 – President Barack Obama's inauguration
January 2009 – Mitchell appointed as the US Middle East envoy
March 2009 – Benjamin Netanyahu elected prime minister
November 2009 – Israel agrees to a ten-month freeze on settlement construction in the West Bank
Spring 2010 – Failure to persuade the parties to resume direct negotiation and agreement to start proximity talks
September 2010 – Direct negotiations begin between the Israelis and Palestinians
26 September 2010 – Direct negotiation suspended.
November 2012 – Obama elected to second term.
July 2013 – The parties agree to renew negotiations on a final status agreement, based on Kerry's plan.
November 2013 – Change of focus to negotiation on a framework agreement.
February 2014 – Change to negotiating document of Principles.
April 1, 2014 – The Palestinians sign UN letters of accession
April 22, 2014 – Fatah-Hamas reconciliation agreement

References

Aggestam, Karin (2002). "Mediating Asymmetrical Conflict." *Mediterranean Politics* 7, 1: 69–91.

Bercovitch, Jacob (2009). "Mediation and Conflict Resolution," in J. Bercovitch, V. Kremenyuk and I. W. Zartman, editors, *The SAGE Handbook of Conflict Resolution*. Thousand Oaks, CA: Sage Publications, 340–357.

Birnbaum, B. and A. Tibon (2014). "The Explosive, Inside Story of How John Kerry Built an Israel-Palestine Peace Plan – and Watched it Crumble." *New Republic*.

Brom, Shlomo (2014). "The American Principles Document: The Negotiations with Israel and the Palestinians." *INSS*, February 9: 515. Accessed at: http://heb.inss.org.il/index.aspx?id=4354&articleid=6593.

Brom, S., U. Dekel and A. Kurtz (2015). "The Israeli Palestinian arena: Lessons following failed negotiation and military conflict." *INSS* 2014–2015. Accessed at: http://heb.inss.org.il/index.aspx?id=4354&articleid=8747.

Channel 2 News (2013). "Celebrations at the Palestinian Authority: An agreement will be signed only when all the prisoners are back." December 13. Accessed at: http://www.mako.co.il/news-military/security/Article-32f7e9beca54341004.htm.

Cohen, G. and J. Khoury (2013). "Thousands protest in front of Ofer Prison against the prisoners' release." *Haaretz*, October 28. Accessed at: http://www.haaretz.co.il/.2151422.

Cohen, Yaacov (2013). "Palestinians resume negotiations and internal audit doubts about his success." The Middle East Media Research Institute, October 13. Accessed at: http://www.memri.org.il/cgiwebaxy/sal/sal.pl?lang=he&ID=875141_memri&act=show&dbid=articles&dataid=3522.

Dekel, U., A. Kurtz and G. Sher (2014). "Israel and the political process-Plan A, Plan B and what is in-between." *INSS* 2013–2014. Tel Aviv University. Accessed at: http://heb.inss.org.il/index.aspx?id=4354&articleid=6455.

Diehl, Jackson (2009). "Abbas's Waiting Game on Peace with Israel." *The Washington Post*, May 29.

Friedman, Uri (2014). "Martin Indyk Explains the Collapse of the Middle East Peace Process." *The Atlantic*, July 3.

Haaretz (2010). "Netanyahu Offers Settlement Freeze in Return for Recognition as Jewish State, Palestinians Say No." October 10. Accessed at: http://www.haaretz.com/israel-news/netanyahu-offers-settlement-freeze-in-return-for-recognition-as-jewish-state-palestinians-say-no-1.318447.

Haaretz (2014). "Obama administration officials are considering releasing Pollard for the extension." April 1. Accessed at: http://www.haaretz.co.il/news/politics/1.2284951.

Halevi, Jonathan D. (2014). "The Crisis in the Peace Talks Was Pre-Planned by the Palestinians." *Jerusalem Center for Public Affairs*, April 10. Accessed at: http://jcpa.org/article/crisis-peace-talks/.

Harel, Amos (2013). "Release of prisoners: the double protection of Netanyahu from escalation in the West Bank and the collapse of talks." *Haaretz*, October 13. Accessed at: http://www.haaretz.co.il/news/politics/.premium-1.2150865.

International Centre for the Study of Radicalisation and Political Violence (2013). "Kerry's joint interview with Israeli and Palestinian reporters: A step forward or a step in the wrong direction?" King's College London, November 12. Accessed at: http://icsr.info/2013/11/kerrys-joint-interview-israeli-palestinian-reporters-step-forward-step-wrong-direction/.

Kalman, Aaron (2013). "Kerry: Israeli 'prosperity' prevents sense of urgency about peace." *The Times of Israel*, May 23. Accessed at: http://www.timesofisrael.com/kerry-israeli-prosperity-preventing-sense-of-urgency-about-peace/.

Kerry, John (2013). "Remarks at the American Jewish Committee Global Forum." US Department of State, June 3. Washington, DC. Accessed at: https://2009–2017.state.gov/secretary/remarks/2013/06/210236.htm.

Kerry, J., T. Livni and S. Erekat (2013). "Remarks on the Middle East Peace Process Talks." US Department of State, July 30. Washington, DC. Accessed at: https://2009-2017.state.gov/secretary/remarks/2013/07/212553.htm.

Kershner, Isabel (2009). "Netanyahu Backs Palestinian State, with Caveats." *The New York Times*, June 14.

Khalidi, Rashid I. (2014). "Chronicles of a Death Foretold." *Journal of Palestinian Studies* 43, 3. Accessed at: http://www.palestine-studies.org/print/jps/fulltext/164336.

Khoury, Jackie (2014). "Senior official in Abbas' bureau: Kerry did not present any new initiative to us for negotiation." *Haaretz*, October 16. Accessed at: http://www.haaretz.co.il/news/politics/.premium-1.2460246.

Kirk, M., M. Wiser and J. Gilmore (2016). "Netanyahu at War." In Public Broadcasting Service, *Frontline*, January 5. Accessed at: http://www.pbs.org/wgbh/frontline/film/netanyahu-at-war

Lakshmanan, I. and N. Gaouette (2013). "Kerry's Day-and-Night Pursuit Reaps Fragile Mideast Talks." *Bloomberg*, July 22. Accessed at: https://www.bloomberg.com/news/articles/2013–07–21/kerry-s-day-and-night-pursuit-reaps-fragile-mideast-talks.

Landler, Mark (2010). "In Middle East Peace Talks, Clinton Faces a Crucial Test." *The New York Times*, September 4.

Landler, M. and M. Gordon (2014). "US Is Weighing Release of a Spy for the Israelis." *The New York Times*, March 31.

Liss, Yehonathan (2013). "Conflict between the torch and storm troopers attacking bent on promoting law against releasing terrorists." *Haaretz*, October 27. Accessed at: http://www.haaretz.co.il/news/politics/1.2150295.

Miller, Aaron D. (2013). "What makes John Kerry think he can secure peace in Israel?" *The Washington Post*, July 25.

Miller, Aaron D. (2016). "Why US diplomacy can't fix the Middle East." *The Washington Post*, June 3.

Mitchell, George J. (2015). *The Negotiator*. New York: Simon and Schuster.

Pruitt, Dean G. (2005). "Whither Ripeness Theory?" *Working paper No. 25*. Washington, DC: George Mason University Press. Accessed at: www.gmu.edu/departments/ICAR/wp_25_pruitt.pdf.

Pruitt, Dean G. (2007). "Readiness Theory and the Northern Ireland Conflict." *American Behavioral Scientist* 50, 11: 1520–1541.

Rabbani, Mouin (2014). "It's Not Over Until It's Over." *Journal of Palestinian Studies* 43, 3.

Ravid, Barak (2013a). "The evening of the prisoners' release: Israel announces the construction of 1,200 units across the Green Line." *Haaretz*, August 11. Accessed at: www.haaretz.co.il/news/politics/1.2094442.

Ravid, Barak (2013b). "All You Wanted to Know about the Resumption of the Israeli-Palestinian Negotiations." *Haaretz*, August 5. Accessed at: http://www.haaretz.co.il/news/whatis/.premium-1.2089027.

Ravid, Barak (2013c). "The Palestinians Rejected the American Proposal for Security Arrangements in a Future Agreement." *Haaretz*, December 5. Accessed: http://www.haaretz.co.il/news/politics/1.2183627.

Ravid, Barak (2014a). "US is Pessimistic about Achieving a Framework Agreement by the End of the Month." *Haaretz*, March 3. Accessed at: http://www.haaretz.co.il/news/politics/.premium-1.2257349.

Ravid, Barak (2014b). "Kerry in a Closed Conversation: Without Peace, Israel is Liable to Become an Apartheid State." *Haaretz*, April 28. Accessed at: http://www.haaretz.co.il/news/politics/1.2306672.

Ravid, Barak (2014c). "Netanyahu's Flexibility, the Americans' Mistake," *Haaretz*, July 5. Accessed at: http://www.haaretz.co.il/israel-peace-convention/1.2359763.

Ravid, B. and J. Khoury (2013). "Netanyahu on the prisoners' release: Important move for the state." *Haaretz*, July 28. Accessed at: www.haaretz.co.il/news/politics/1.2082262.

Ravid, B. and J. Khoury (2014). "Kerry to Meet with Abbas Today in Effort to Prevent Breakdown of Negotiations." *Haaretz*, March 24. Accessed at: http://www.haaretz.co.il/news/politics/1.2279728.

Rosen, Steven J. (2010). "Interesting George Mitchell Interview." *Middle East Forum*, January 7.

Rudoren, Jodi (2014). "Palestinians Set to Seek Redress in a World Court." *The New York Times*, December 31.

Ross, Dennis B. (2015). "Stop Giving Palestinians a Pass." *The New York Times*, January 5.

Schiff, Amira (2014). "Reaching a Mutual Agreement: Readiness Theory and Coalition Building in the Aceh Peace Process." *Negotiation and Conflict Management Research* 7, 1: 57–82.

Segal, Udi (2013a). "This is how the prisoners deal was struck in return for construction." *Channel 2 News*, October 30. Accessed at: www.mako.co.il/news-columns/Article-3cd4495b1ca0241004.html.

Segal, Udi (2013b). "Netanyahu in a letter on the release of the prisoners: Prime Ministers are required to make decisions that go against public opinion." *Channel 2 News*, July 27. Accessed at: http://www.mako.co.il/newsmilitary/israel/Article62e00844ae02041004.htm.

Sherwood, Harriet (2013). "Kerry: Two years left to reach two-state solution in Middle East peace process." *The Guardian*, April 18. Accessed at: https://www.theguardian.com/world/2013/apr/18/kerry-two-state-solution-middle-east.

Tibon, Amir (2014a). "Will He Close a Deal? Kerry to Meet with Netanyahu and Abu Mazen." *Walla News*, March 31. Accessed at: http://news.walla.co.il/item/2734078.

Tibon, Amir (2014b). "The UN Security Council Rejected the Palestinian Proposal." *Walla News*, December 31. Accessed at: http://news.walla.co.il/item/2815391.

Touval, S. and I. W. Zartman (2001). "International Mediation in the Post-Cold War Era," in C. A. Crocker, F. O. Hampson and P. Aall, editors, *Turbulent Peace: The Challenges of Managing International Conflict.* Washington, DC: US Institute of Peace Press.

Tzena, Shlomo (2013). "Bennett on the prisoner release: Can live with that." *Israel Hayom*, November 1. Accessed at: www.israelhayom.co.il/article/128703.

Yaar, E. and T. Hermann (2014a). *The Peace Index*, January. Accessed at: http://www.peaceindex.org/indexMonthEng.aspx?num=273&monthname=January.

Yaar, E. and T. Hermann (2014b). *Peace Index Column*, February. Accessed at: http://www.idi.org.il/media/3091381/Peace_Index_February_2014-Eng.pdf.

Yadlin, Amos (2014). "Focus on the Essence, Not on the Process." *Maariv Online*, August 6. Accessed at: http://www.maariv.co.il/landedpages/printarticle.aspx?id=441893.

Zanany, Omer (2015). *Annapolis Process (2007–2008): Oasis or Mirage.* Tel Aviv: Tami Steinmetz Center for Peace Research, Tel Aviv University.

Zartman, I. William (1999). *Negotiations as a Mechanism for Resolution in the Arab-Israeli Conflict.* Jerusalem: The Leonard Davis Institute, The Hebrew University of Jerusalem.

Zartman, I. William (2000). "The Hurting Stalemate and Beyond," in P. C. Stern and D. Druckman, editors, *Conflict Resolution after the Cold War.* Washington D.C.: National Academy Press.

Zartman, I. William (2008). "Ripeness Revisited: The Push and Pull of Conflict Management," in William I. Zartman, editor, *Essays on Theory and Practice.* New York: Routledge.

Zartman, I. William (2012). "Process Reasons for Failure," in Guy Olivier Faure, editor, *Unfinished Business: Why International Negotiations Fail.* Athens, GA: University of Georgia Press.

Zartman, I. W. and A. deSoto (2010). *Timing Mediation Initiatives.* Washington, DC: United States Institute of Peace Press.

Zartman, I. W. and J. Z. Rubin (2000). *Power and Negotiation.* Ann Arbor, MI: University of Michigan Press.

Getting the Job Done: Bolstering American Mediation on Palestine. An Israeli Plan for American Mediation of the Israeli-Palestinian Conflict

Galia Golan
Department of Political Science, Hebrew University of Jerusalem, Jerusalem, Israel
ggolan@idc.ac.il

Received 21 February 2016; accepted 20 July 2017

Abstract

Inasmuch as the 2015 Israeli elections brought to power a Netanyahu-led coalition even more ideologically opposed to the creation of a Palestinian state than the previous coalitions, the absence of political will to reach agreement would appear to prejudge the outcome of any future negotiations should they take place. For this reason, recommendations to improve American mediation efforts remain in the realm of theory, but nevertheless may provide useful suggestions for the more basic step of returning the sides to serious negotiations.

Keywords

Israeli-Palestinian conflict – mediation – United States

* Galia Golan is Darwin Professor emerita of the Hebrew University of Jerusalem where she was Chair of the Political Science Department. A leading Israeli analyst and peace activist, her most recent book is *Israeli Peacemaking since 1967: Factors Behind the Breakthroughs and Failures* (Abingdon: Routledge, 2014).

 | DOI:10.1163/9789004393295_004

The title "An Israeli Plan" may be misleading. There are different views regarding what is "pro-Israel," and in Israel itself there are very different views of what is good, even vital, for Israel's future. I think I can say I am representative of a public that believes that the occupation – and the conflict – must end if Israel is to stop the descent down the slippery slope to apartheid, and that the only *solution* is that of two independent states, Israel and Palestine, side by side. While in the end, everything depends upon the leaders and publics of both the Israelis and the Palestinians, past experience and present circumstances indicate that outside help is needed – even if only in the form of pressure that helps the respective leaders "sell" an agreement to their own publics.

With regard to Israel, there is no doubt that this would be an easier task if the government were in the hands of a right-wing leader, who could then count on the support of the opposition parties to make peace, as was the case in the 1979 peace agreement with Egypt. But this would mean a right-wing leadership that saw the necessity of an agreement, as was the case to some degree at least, with past right-wing leaders: Menachem Begin, Ariel Sharon and Ehud Olmert. This is unlikely to happen today. Former Foreign Minister[1] Tzipi Livny is the closest to this "model" in that she, like Olmert (despite enormous differences between the two) moved from the heart of the historic right-wing to an understanding of the need to end the occupation. In the case of Livny, she moved even to the point of joining with the Labor party for the 2015 elections. Like Sharon and Olmert's Kadima party (and Rabin's Labor Party before them), the new Herzog (Labor)-Livny list, called the "Zionist camp," employed the "demographic argument" unashamedly in the 2015 elections.

For these leaders and most Israelis, the threat of a bi-national state, in which Jews would eventually become a minority, is seen as a threat greater than that of war from beyond the borders. To the demographic argument, they add a warning of the alternative, namely international isolation and the risk of losing even US support if Israel does not move toward a solution. Indeed, the need for continued US support, in the form of guarantees for our future security as well as political needs, may well prove to be the crucial factor in the eyes of the Israeli security and political establishments – and possibly also the public.

The most important concern among Israeli leaders since the founding of the state, and one inculcated into and shared by the Israeli public, is that of the so-called existential threat to the country based on fear that our legitimacy as a state – in this region – has not and will not be accepted. This issue of legitimacy lies at the center of the all-encompassing concern for security and

1 Olmert's successor as head of Kadima and later head of her own newer party, Hatnuah.

an over-riding mistrust of the enemy. In practice, it has meant a preference for what at various times have been considered essential military measures over – indeed instead of – peace. Any peace effort, and mediation, must bear this in mind and find a way to deal with it. Thus, involvement of social and political psychologists in the preparatory stage of the mediation effort might be helpful.[2]

Beyond the crucial element of mistrust, the current deadlock has a number of sources, the first and most important being the absence of interest, i.e., political will, on the part of the Netanyahu government to reach a peace agreement (ending the occupation and creation of a viable Palestinian state) due to both ideological and political factors. The result, for example, as seen in the Kerry-led talks of 2014–15, was the addition of Israeli demands for explicit Palestinian recognition of the Jewish nature of the State of Israel and pressure to determine the final security measures before discussion of where and what borders were to be secured. Finally, there was also the Israeli failure to implement steps originally set as conditions for opening the negotiations (the final stage of the release of prisoners – which had been agreed upon as a substitute for the Palestinian demand for a settlement freeze). It seems likely that a stalemate would have been reached anyway in the Kerry negotiations, due, for example, to disagreement over territorial swap percentages, or possible Palestinian resistance to concessions on Jerusalem or the Israeli insistence upon IDF troops in the Jordan Rift Valley or other demands. A basic mistake appears to have been Kerry's willingness to incorporate Israeli demands before conveying his plan to the Palestinians. In addition, unlike Kissinger in 1974–75, Kerry did not appear to have the full authority of the White House needed in order to bring pressure on Jerusalem.

Inasmuch as the 2015 Israeli elections brought to power a Netanyahu-led coalition even more ideologically opposed to the creation of a Palestinian state than the previous coalitions, the absence of a political will to reach agreement would appear to prejudge the outcome of any future negotiations should they take place. Moreover, the election of Trump in the United States has strengthened the more ambitious extremists in the present Israeli government (viz. the open demands for annexation of the West Bank and the renunciation of the two-state solution by members of the coalition). For these reasons, recommendations to improve American mediation efforts remain in the realm of theory but, nevertheless, they may provide useful suggestions for the more basic step

2 Carter had biographical and psychological analyses of Sadat and Begin prepared for his study prior to his departure for Camp David in 1978. Rabin studied Sadat's biography in depth prior to his talks with the Egyptians in 1974.

of returning the sides to serious negotiations. That said, the elections in the United States have added a wild card to the deck – and unknown factor that may defy application of any of the lessons learned from past American mediation efforts in this conflict. In the absence of a coherent Trump administration foreign policy or strategy for the Middle East, one may only assume that the consultations by While House emissaries Kushner and Greenblatt with the Israeli and Palestinian leaders have been meant to pave the wave for resumption of negotiations. Inasmuch as President Trump has said that the US will play a role in such talks, whether as mediator or facilitator or other role, and that the result will be the "ultimate deal," our comments on "getting the job done" may be relevant.

Assumptions

Certain assumptions may be taken into account with regard to this latter task as well as to future US mediation.[3] The first assumption for the near future is that the US has a strategic interest in an Israeli-Palestinian peace agreement inasmuch as an end to this conflict would contribute to the US effort to regain both influence and stability in the region. The conflict fuels at least the motivation of extremist elements, while limiting US options with regard to the various countries in the region, moderate and militant alike, and the possibilities for more successful cooperation with allies in the region (Turkey, Saudi Arabia). The key regarding this regional interest is the degree to which Washington's friends in the region need cooperation with Israel in the present struggles in the Gulf and against Iran – at the expense of the Palestinians.

Secondly, President Trump has neither the qualifications nor the inclinations to take a genuine mediator role similar to that of former presidents Carter or Clinton. Touting his intention (and presumed ability) to reach "the ultimate deal," he has already made it clear that his former lawyer Greenblatt and his son-in-law Kushner will be conducting talks that he, Trump, wishes to see take place. To this equation one must add, however, Trump's ego. Will ego considerations lead him to abandon negotiations if they appear to be heading for failure? Or would he be willing to bring significant pressure on Israel to make the concessions necessary for a successful negotiation? It is difficult to make any assumption on this point. Trump's own inclinations (so far as they have appeared thus far), his family and White House associates, along with

3 My comments and suggestions regarding US mediation relate mainly to dealing with the Israeli side.

both the overwhelming majority of both Republican and Democratic members of Congress, all tend to rule against such pressure. Less dependent upon American Jewish diaspora approval than almost any of his predecessors, Trump has no reason to be concerned over diaspora opposition to a use of pressure on Netanyahu. The only factor that might, nonetheless, encourage Trump's use of pressure would be the ego element – to get the "deal" rather than walk away, particularly if other initiatives falter or the cases connected with Russian interference in the 2016 elections become still more problematic for him.

Thirdly, one must assume a sorely divided Israeli government coalition propelled by Netanyahu's rivalry with the still more rightwing Naftali Bennet, with both leaders' struggling to maintain support from their settler bases. The very entry of this government to negotiations would be the result of a coalition battle leading to certain compromises and commitments on Netanyahu's part in order to proceed (which he would do only to placate Trump). The dissent within the government will be accompanied by vocal, possibly strong, opposition within the Israeli public (and also the Palestinian, for different reasons).

Framework Options

There are a number of options for the framework of the mediation, beginning with the familiar shuttle diplomacy model of the Kissinger and recent Kerry efforts. Other formats employed by the US were direct bilateral Israeli-Palestinian (or Israeli-Syrian) talks with the United States participating as occasional mediator in the person of the secretary of state or lower level US facilitators, for example, in the Annapolis process. An additional option is the successful Camp David 1978 model of direct mediation by the US President himself. Broader frameworks have been tried, usually under UN auspices, beginning with the Geneva Conference of 1973, then the 1991 Madrid Conference and most recently the Annapolis Conference of 2007. All of these were basically opening sessions followed by direct bilateral (and multilateral) talks; the post-Madrid talks took place without US mediation. The Annapolis framework was the broadest, including most Arab states and implicitly based on the Arab Peace Initiative of 2002. The regional, multi-lateral framework is an option that holds promise for American efforts to strength bonds with the moderate Sunni Arab states, and it has the advantage of providing direct Israeli negotiations with Saudi Arabia and possibly other Arab states besides Egypt and Jordan. Israel has long sought relationships with the other Arab states that are not conditioned upon resolution of the Palestinian issue. This position appears to have

Trump's support and, given Saudi and others' interests in (and need for) cooperation with Israel in intelligence and other security matters in their struggle against the Shia and specifically Iran, Israel may believe it can go the regional route without conceding anything regarding the Palestinians. Indeed, there are signs that this is the case, though not admitted publicly by the Saudis or others.

Procedural Options for US in Negotiations

Whatever procedures or steps are chosen, it would be wise to follow a basic guideline set by President Carter at Camp David 1978, namely, total secrecy regarding the content and progress of the negotiations. Exclusion of the press and prevention of leaks, to the degree possible, can reduce outside interference, in particular attempts by spoilers to derail the talks. One need only recall the leak of an American document during the critical Israeli-Syrian talks of January 2000, possibly initiated by the Israeli prime minister Ehud Bark as a trial balloon or even with the intention of spoiling, that embarrassed the Syrians to the point of disrupting the talks altogether (Golan 2014: 79–86; Kibrik & Kornberg 2018; Sagie 2011).

The US has a number of procedural options for the talks, representing varying degrees of involvement (or possibly commitment). Three of these would indicate the direction to be taken, for example, (1) US presentation of its own parameters for a final agreement or (2) presentation of the Arab Peace Initiative (or a UNSC resolution that may have been adopted with specific parameters), or (3) presentation of the Clinton Parameters and Abu Mazen-Olmert understandings, as a basis for the talks. All of these appear unlikely in view of the White House's affinity for Netanyahu's government and, more importantly perhaps, the need to reject the approaches of Trump's predecessors. Alternatively, the US might simply present, at the outset, its own views of the interests, concerns, and positions of the two sides as a starting point for talks. A far more limited, but more likely, role would be restricting the American involvement to providing bridging proposals in the course of the talks, and/or compromise formulations, side letters, bi-lateral memoranda of understanding, and the like. Memoranda of Understanding (MOU) were particularly helpful in the 1975 Israel-Egypt Interim Agreement; compromise formulae and side letters were helpful in the 1978 Camp David talks, especially to provide for acceptance by the Knesset in the face of Israeli spoilers. However, ambiguity, for the sake of agreement, must also be avoided since it can, and in the past did, cause misunderstanding (or deception) on such matters, for example, as a settlement freeze. Other matters were left open, due to Israeli unwillingness to make firm commitments (for example, a timetable for implementation of the autonomy plan), and therefore never implemented. The avoidance of difficult issues should be minimized – primarily to avoid future disputes and if a genuine agreement is to be reached and honored.

US mediators may, of course, adopt a combination of the various procedures, but criticism of America's role in the past has pointed to the need for a direct, pro-active role, beyond mere facilitation through bridging proposals and the like (Kurtzer et al. 2013).

Challenges US Mediators Will Face

Regional and International Environment

A major challenge to negotiations for a final settlement is the instability and even chaos raging in the region today. Be it the expanding violence of ISIL and other Islamist groups, the armed conflict in Yemen, the near collapse of Iraq, the civil war in Syria, and even the domestic disarray in Egypt, including violence inside Sinai, there is little to assuage Israeli concerns over the durability and trustworthiness of any agreement that may reached with the Arabs. Nor, in Israeli eyes, could an agreement be dependent upon third parties to ensure future security (and thus justify the abandonment of certain types of deal-breaking security measures sought in the past, such as continued Israeli control of Palestine's eastern border).

Yet these very challenges, daunting and important as they may be, may also provide something of an advantage – or opportunity. At least so far as Israel is concerned, developments in the region have created a mutuality of interests with major Arab states. Whereas in the recent past such a mutuality could be detected in the hostility toward or fears regarding Iran, the newer threats, particularly of ISIL, provide a strong incentive and possibly an opportunity for cooperation. This would include incentive for assistance to US efforts (on the Israeli-Arab track) from America's regional allies, Saudi Arabia, Jordan, and Egypt (assuming restoration of Washington's formerly close relationship with Cairo). The question, as already noted, is how loyal these Arab allies will be to the Palestinians in view of the possibly more urgent need for cooperation with Israel.

Beyond the region, circumstances may be somewhat advantageous insofar as the EU, despite its other pressing concerns, appears increasingly willing to press Israel, possibly even by means of boycotts or sanctions, to negotiate seriously for an agreement with the Palestinians. Freed of much of its past deference to Washington and American positions, the Europeans may now be more willing to take such steps. And UNSC resolution 2334 provides a basis for doing so, given the clause calling for strictly maintaining the distinction between the territory of the state of Israel and the occupied territories.

Political/Psychological Challenges on the Israeli Side

The major concern of Israelis – the public as well as leadership – over the increasing activity of ISIL and other Islamist extremists close to Israel's borders has fortified deep-seated insecurities and fears. These fears, often nurtured and manipulated by right-wing Israeli governments, are then linked to Israelis' historic and pervasive mistrust of the Arabs, providing a serious challenge to outside efforts at peacemaking. At the core is uncertainty over the acceptance of Israel, its legitimacy (i.e., Jewish rights), in the region. The general belief that there is "no partner" on the other side (the "no Arab leader will ever make genuine peace with us" mantra expressed for example by Yitzhak Rabin in 1974 or Netanyahu's insistence on Palestinian recognition of the Jewish character of Israel) are manifestations of this, strengthened by the failures of past negotiations and Palestinian violence. These attitudes are also apparent in the mistrust regarding security arrangements in whatever deal is to be made. (The poor record of UN peacekeeping has not helped in overcoming this challenge.)

Other aspects of a possible agreement also provide serious challenges. Israeli opposition to compromise on the refugee issue, particularly to allowing that there is a *right* of return, even in principle, derives from the suspicion that this would open the flood-gates, leading eventually to an Arab majority inside Israel itself. The result would be a bi-national state, in which, at best, Jews would be a minority once again. Jerusalem too is an issue that offers psychological as well as political challenges. Historic, religious and emotional attachments to all of Jerusalem, though particularly the Temple Mount in East Jerusalem, are generally real. They have been nurtured and manipulated by most Israeli governments, but increasingly so by the present coalition with its nationalist-religious bias and increasing assaults on secularism in the country. For many, Jerusalem has become (or for some always was) the symbol of Jewish legitimacy in this place, in this region.

As problematic as all these challenges may be, the greatest challenge is most likely to be a very concrete one: the need to evacuate thousands, possibly even tens of thousands of Jewish settlers from their homes in the West Bank. Even relocation to other settlements within areas to be annexed by Israel will not be an easy matter since many of the settlements likely to be evacuated are among the more extreme ideological ones.[4] Indeed, the official settler movement – with support from the government coalition's extremist party Habayit Hayehudi (Jewish Home) – may mobilize to oppose any evacuation. The experiences of Gush Katif (disengagement from the Gaza Strip, 2005), and, later, various outposts in the West Bank, have demonstrated that increasing numbers of settlers may be willing to resist by force. There could be an additional problem of religious, settler soldiers and officers (whose numbers have grown in the regular army) refusing to carry out evacuation orders. In any case, scenes of Israeli soldiers fighting Jewish settlers is not one the government wishes to see, and the potential for civil war is something the settler movement can be expected to emphasize prior to or during negotiations. That said, studies have shown that large portions of the settler population can be persuaded to leave willingly if approached in an appropriate psychological and political manner (Hirsch-Hoeffler et al. 2018). The risk, however, will have to be weighed by the government, and the settler movement can be expected to threaten if not actually carry out a civil war in order to stay the government's hand in negotiations.

Additional challenges will come from other opponents, even within the Israeli leadership or leading parties, that is, parties in the ruling coalition. Right-wing governments have managed over the years to introduce legislation that limits the ability of a leader to make peace if it entails conceding any territory. Thus, there will also be the challenge of winning over sufficient support within the Knesset, particularly in the likely case that the governing coalition is divided.

Political/Psychological Challenges on the Palestinian Side

There will be a major political challenge on the Palestinian side as well, inasmuch as Abu Mazen has become increasingly dictatorial, alienating past colleagues and supporters, and losing his political base. This situation is aggravated by the disarray that has continued within the ruling Fatah Party for years, with divisions, defections, rivalries and sometimes chaos. Hamas has been

4 The people in the settlements near the green line – settlements often called bedroom communities, are generally less ideologically motivated. Indeed the majority of settlers are "quality of life" settlers who merely responded to economic incentives to move to the West Bank (this includes a minority of new immigrants as well). With proper compensation for relocation (if living outside the blocs), many of this type of setter will not resist though they might fall into the category of "greedy spoilers" seeking to gain greater compensation. (Various types of spoilers have been identified, see notably Stedman's categorization (1997) of "total," "limited" and "greedy" spoilers. The Israeli NGO Blue and White, has produced calculations regarding the costs of moving and compensating settlers.

gaining strength in the West Bank (as distinct from Gaza, where they are the ruling party), along with extremist Islamist elements. While Hamas does not have majority support (Palestinian Policy and Survey Research Center 2015), the public is disappointed in the Palestinian Authority and Fatah, and disillusioned with the non-violent path advocated by Abu Mazen. The failure of past negotiations has strengthened this disillusionment, while Hamas is viewed by many as having continued the resistance, even successfully, since Hamas violence is credited with forcing Israel out of Gaza in 2005.

A further challenge on the Palestinian side is the popular belief, of the majority of Palestinians, that Israel is not a partner for peace. The general view is that Israel – regardless of whatever party is in power – has no intention of ending the occupation and leaving the West Bank (or relinquishing control over Gaza from outside). This view is substantiated and fortified by Israel's continued expansion of settlement building, in East Jerusalem as well as the West Bank. The addition of further conditions, such as the Netanyahu demand for recognition of the Jewish character of the state of Israel, the return to past security demands (in the Jordan valley, for example) believed to have been overcome in the past, along with negative public statements by Israeli leaders and the increasing political strength of the extreme right in Israel, all strengthen these views among the Palestinians.

A further challenge to the Americans, specifically, is the conviction that the US is not an "honest broker." Rather, the US is viewed as a solid and loyal ally of Israel, representing Israeli positions and striving only to satisfy Jerusalem, and also Israel's powerful supporters in the US Congress. All of this, in the eyes of most Palestinians, is evidenced by repeated US backing for Israel in international fora, in particular American opposition to Palestinian membership in the UN and pressure on US allies to refrain from recognizing the Palestinian state or offering a new UNSC resolution that might bring pressure on Israel – even in the Obama period. The strong right wing (pro-Netanyahu and pro-settlements) leanings of Trump's appointees and financial backers merely fortify this view.

Potential Spoilers

Reference has already been made to some spoilers, but given their great potential – as proven in the past and most tragically in the Oslo period, American mediators should view them as an important category in themselves (Golan & Sher 2018; Stedman 1997; Ellman et al. 2014: 36; Newman & Richmond 2006: 59–77; Haklai 2003; Seliktar 2002: 119–149). On the Israeli side, the extreme right-wing parties within the government coalition, particularly the nationalist-religious *Jewish Home* party led by Naftali Bennet – as well as individuals in the Likud party itself – can be expected to try to impede peace efforts, including discrediting US efforts and mediators. In this they will be joined (or led) by the organized settler movement, a core of ideologically dedicated, mostly religious, diehards who can garner some support from the religious-Zionist community within Israel. They may be joined by the less ideologically motivated settler constituency consisting of people simply interested in keeping their homes and benefits. The use of violence cannot be ruled out and can be expected at least from the small settler groups associated with terrorism and vandalism, often under the name of "price tag" reprisal attacks.

Settler spoilers can also be expected to engage the Jewish diaspora, particularly inside the United States. These would include AIPAC, and, in the Trump era, the increasingly more vocal and more right-wing Zionist Organization of America, as well as other influential (and wealthy) Jewish groups and individuals. While the US diaspora is more divided today (on an organizational basis) than it was in the Oslo period, the conservative wing is still strong – and linked to a more powerful Republican political base than in previous times. The issue might boil down to the degree to which a settler-opposed agreement is nonetheless reached and supported by Trump. (Bear in mind that the negotiations are being conducted by American negotiators who, like Trump himself, have contributed to and support the settler movement.)

Spoilers on the Palestinian side will be no less problematic. Given the widespread disillusionment and skepticism among the public, the potential for spoiler activity is high. The more moderate but serious spoiling activity may come from the organized NGO community in the West Bank which has spearheaded an anti-normalization campaign against cooperation even with the Israeli peace camp. They may campaign against trusting US mediation and any bilateral agreement with Israel. Their arguments may well resonate with the increasing number of young people who have joined the ranks of the disillusioned. Spoiling action may be expected from the small, more radical parties (mainly the PFLP), but more important spoilers might come from within Fatah itself (adversaries of Abu Mazen, supporters perhaps of the deposed former security chief Mohammed Dahlan, for example). The most dangerous – and potentially effective – spoilers, as evidenced in the Oslo period, will come from Hamas, the Islamic Jihad and other extremist Islamist groups. Today there is the newer threat of terrorism from global groups such as ISIL and al-Qaeda, not necessarily connected with the Palestinian groups but potentially critical spoilers nonetheless.

Aside from specific tactics that may be employed to minimize spoiler action during negotiations (discussed below), it is important that the mediators project not only trustworthiness but also conviction and perseverance in the face of such actions. Spoiling may come, however, from the leaders or negotiators themselves, unintentionally perhaps but also intentionally (what have been called "devious actors") (Newman & Richmond 2006; Kibrik & Kornberg 2018).[5] Mediators must be alert to such spoilers, and employ the various measures available to cope with them, such as the "departing train" tactic and others.

Past experience has shown that a gradual approach of partial and/or interim agreements, such as economic steps and confidence building measures, may be helpful. These have been suggested by the Trump administration. However, so long as the occupation continues, such steps cannot bring the lasting quiet or trust. It may be remembered that the first intifada broke out at a time of relative economic satisfaction in the West Bank. Moreover, economic steps (a so-called "economic peace", which is the preferred direction for Netanyahu and possibly Trump), cannot in themselves constitute peace so long as Israel maintains the occupation. In addition, as demonstrated by the Oslo Accords, an interim agreement merely provides time and opportunity for spoilers to organize and mobilize, impeding and even defeating the process. The absence of an "end game," that is, a lack of clarity as to what is ultimately to be achieved, serves potential spoilers, feeding the fears of the skeptics. The publics on both sides must have a clear view of the goal – along the lines that are of greatest interest to them: for the Palestinians, that the occupation will end and an independent Palestinian state will be created; for the Israelis, that the conflict and all claims will end and Israeli relations with the Arab world will be opened. The attractiveness of the goal – as well as the conviction that it can and will be attained – is needed in order to justify the perceived sacrifices that will have to be made. Sacrifices, on the Israeli side: giving up tangible assets, namely land, and, more concretely still, evacuating settlers with all that such a task entails financially, politically, psychologically. On the Palestinian side: giving up both sovereignty in 78% of Palestine and the return of all the refugees to their original places of residence.

Tactics during Negotiations

The period of negotiations is critical not only to achieve an agreement – obviously the goal of the talks – but also to achieve an agreement that can be accepted and implemented by both sides. This will be no small feat, given the asymmetry of the protagonists, but it may be the most important task of the

5 To this day, it is not clear if Barak was a devious actor or an unintentional spoiler, or if he became the former only in the negotiating process.

US mediators. Based on past experience in Israeli/Arab negotiations as well as that of other conflicts, the following are tactical steps that the US might take to deal with the challenges mentioned above:

1. Involve respected pro-peace diaspora figures as go-betweens Israel and the US Administration, as well as between the US Administration and the Congress.
2. Involve and actively pursue consultation with Arab states such as Saudi Arabia as well as Jordan and Egypt.
3. Arrange gestures to each side, such as local televised appearances (if not actually live visits) by leaders from the opposing side and also from Arab states, especially Saudi Arabia if possible (FRUS 1975).[6]
4. Meet quietly with political elites of both sides, including potential spoilers.
5. Appear publicly to audiences of each side (depending on time framework).[7]
6. Mediate secret meeting(s) between Israeli and Arab leaders (track 1½).
7. Meet with civil society leaders (including religious leaders) and media on each side and, so far as possible, with potential spoilers (secret or open meetings) as well.
8. Engage supporters from civil society (preferably individuals or groups of former opponents to an agreement) both in the US and among the protagonists (Israel and Palestine), either outside the negotiations or even by inclusion of a representative in the negotiations themselves.[8]
9. Organize secret track two/ADR with "limited" spoilers (skeptics, especially within political parties of each side).

Aside from these efforts to deal with challenges and spoilers, it would be wise to address the negotiating approach itself. Thus, the US might try to focus negotiations on the need to meet the *interests* of the two sides, avoiding the past Israeli attitude that the land is all "ours" and negotiations are merely meant to decide how much land Israel is willing to "give" to the Palestinians. This is an attitude linked to conflicting narratives and identity – matters which are

6 Rabin's 1974 personal letter to Sadat regarding the sincerity of his intention to reach peace was a US inspired gesture that helped lead Sadat to greater efforts to find a solution for Israeli demands.

7 If Camp David type meeting, then this may not be relevant during negotiations.

8 According to Hoffman (2015), "A recent examination of 83 peace agreements in 40 countries from 1989–2004 found that peace is 60% less likely to fail when both civil society actors and political parties participate in the process."

generally irresolvable. The Palestinians have much the same attitude, but they consider their demand for only 22% of mandated Palestine sufficient compromise. Ignoring this (the PLO's "historic compromise" of 1988), Israel has approached negotiations in the past as a "give and take," expecting (further) Palestinian compromises in exchange for Israeli compromises in a "tit for tat" approach. Such an approach belies the asymmetry of the two sides as well as the PLO's past major concession.

In addition, the US may facilitate agreement, as already suggested, by proposing appendices, side letters, and alternate wording for difficult issues or clauses, as done so successfully at Camp David. However, a more promising tactic may be to actually present a US plan with a strict timetable or at least clear guideposts and parameters. Beyond this, US incentives will undoubtedly be important if not critical, in the form of US economic-financial support for both sides, along with political and increased military support for Israel. The Arab states should be involved in the incentives to the Palestinians; the Europeans may be mobilized as well. Possibly the most important commitment the Americans can give is an offer of US guarantees, similar to those of the MOU provided for the 1975 Egyptian-Israeli Interim Agreement and the Exchange of Letters provided in connection with the Egyptian-Israeli Framework of Principles, 1978. Obviously, the promise of guarantees goes beyond tactics to an integral part of the agreement itself.

However, if these incentives and the above-mentioned tactics are not sufficient, the US may need to apply pressure or "coercive diplomacy." This could take the form of warnings or threats to the more recalcitrant negotiating side regarding not only the loss of the opportunity for peace, but also the loss of US support (actual or future) if the talks fail. Obviously, this is easier for the US mediator to do with regard to the PLO than to Israel, given the US-Israel relationship and domestic American politics. But it also carries less weight with the PLO than Israel, since the PLO has potential alternatives to the relatively limited US support it receives, while Israel is dependent upon US military assistance as well as other financial and political aid. Such a threat *vis a vis* Israel (the stronger party) would go a long way toward leveling the playing field and thereby improve the chances for achieving a mutually acceptable agreement. It might also convince the PLO that the US is an honest broker, and thus possibly impact Palestinian negotiating positions. Moreover, pressure of this kind may also be the key to moving Israel to a more conciliatory position since this would constitute a tangible – and intolerable – loss for Israel, more compelling (and possibly easier to convey domestically in Israel) than the more amorphous Israeli concern over the demographic or moral consequences of continuing the occupation.

The Issues

If the American mediators are to do more than merely facilitate talks and, rather, strive to bring about an agreement, they will have to at least envisage positions or solutions regarding the issues.

Borders

The issue of Israel's eastern border with the State of Palestine depends, for the Israelis, on the largest number of West Bank settlers who can be accommodated within settlement blocs annexed to Israel;[9] for the Palestinians, it depends upon contiguity of territory and the possibility of claiming that they have not given up any of the territory meant for their "mini-state" (the 22% of mandated Palestine agreed to by the PLO in 1988).[10] To meet Israeli "needs" the principle of land swaps has been accepted (and incorporated into the API) though the PLO demands that swaps be equal and agreed upon.

At the July 2000 Camp David talks, Israel spoke of retaining 9–12% of the West Bank (figures varied during the talks) with a 9:1 swap (a small area southeast of the Gaza Strip would constitute the 1 sq. kilometer to be given the Palestinians). At the later Taba talks, Barak authorized his negotiators to go as low as retaining 8% for Israel; the Clinton Parameters spoke of 3–5% (various references by Clinton) with equal swaps. Olmert and Abu Mazen – according to both their accounts – were close to agreement: Olmert proposed retention of 6.3–6.5% of the West Bank, with 5.8% accommodated via swaps; Abu Mazen proposed 1.9%. The area to be allotted for safe passage (a road or tunnel

9 All negotiations since 1993 assumed Israeli withdrawal from Gaza (although previously, June 1967; Camp David 1978) Israel sought to continue control of Gaza. The dispute over territory revolves around the West Bank, as it has since 1967.

10 While the Israeli government considers the West Bank under belligerent occupation, for the purpose of negotiations, the Israel Foreign Ministry relates to the West Bank as disputed territory. The reasoning: the 1947 UN partition plan (UNGA 181) for the end of the British mandate over Palestine accorded the West Bank and other areas for "an Arab state in Palestine" and the rest for "a Jewish state in Palestine." In the course of the 1948 war, Israel conquered part of the area designated for the Arab state, Jordan conquered the remainder, namely the West Bank, and annexed it shortly thereafter. No country recognized Israel's annexation of the territory acquired and thus Israel never had a recognized eastern border (until part of it in the south was regulated in the Israeli Jordanian peace agreement of 1994). Since Jordan's annexation of the West Bank was recognized only by Great Britain and Pakistan, the Israel Foreign Ministry claims that there was in fact no sovereign and therefore the land is disputed. Further, in 1988 Jordan gave up its claim to the West Bank (in favor of the Palestinians represented by the PLO).

from Gaza to the West Bank) was not to be included but variations in the percentages revolved around such things as "no man's land," the Latrun area and possibly some environs of Jerusalem. Abu Mazen based his figure on the actual constructed area of existing settlements (in 2008) although this figure varies in Israeli reports (Herzog 2011).[11] Olmert based his figure on the accommodation of roughly 80% of the settlers (exclusive of settlers in East Jerusalem).

The unofficial, track-two Geneva Initiative proposed an additional uninhabited area south of Jerusalem for the swaps. Zippi Livni has stated in the past that the present route of the fence/wall should be the future border; this would entail annexing 10% of the West Bank. The crucial area in this (and in the Olmert/Abu Mazen talks) was the large settlement of Ariel, which juts into the West Bank, irrespective of settlement blocs. Recent estimates by Barak's former negotiation team chief, Col. (ret) Shaul Arieli, set 3–4% as the maximum area that could be found for the swaps. Thus, the lower end of the Clinton Parameters, in the area of 3%, possibly slightly more, plus equal swaps remains the most likely option.

Security

Although the Olmert-Abu Mazen talks were conducted on the principle that "nothing is agreed until everything is agreed," both leaders claim that the security issue (only) was "finalized." Israel would be permitted just two early warning posts, on the heights in the center of the West Bank (Ba'al Hazor and Har Eval) and Palestine could have an early warning post in the northern Israeli town of Safed. Use of the electromagnetic field and airspace over the West Bank was apparently worked out. Palestine would be a "non-militarized" state, with only a strong security force for law enforcement.[12] The most controversial issue, finally worked out, revolved around control of the Palestinian border with Jordan. From the first week after the 1967 war, Israel declared the Jordan River as its own border and demanded sovereignty over the Jordan Rift Valley adjacent to it. The rationale was the need for Israeli control in case of invasion by a third army (Iraq or Syria) even if there were a peace agreement (with Jordan or a Palestinian entity). Yitzhak Rabin continued to adhere to this demand, although he admitted to Clinton that changes in warfare and military doctrine (following the first Gulf War and the use of long-range rockets) reduced the need for a military presence on the ground (Clinton 2005: 545).

11 At Camp David the Palestinians presented a map which accorded Israel 2.5% of the West Bank but this included roads leading from Israel proper to the settlement (blocs).

12 There were other clauses allowing for right of pursuit by Israeli military, non-intervention of third forces, and other similar safeguards.

Rabin was rumored to have considered the idea of a 30-year lease of the area for Israel; Barak spoke of no more than a 12-year military presence (Sher 2006: 34–35, 53).[13] Olmert and Abu Mazen finally put this issue to rest, agreeing to the Clinton Parameters' idea of an international force, now specified as a NATO force under US command, to be placed on the border, possibly on the Jordanian side. (Secretary C. Rice spoke to the NATO commander about this option, though Livni adhered to the former demand for an Israeli military presence (Swisher & Karmi 2011: 189)).

Netanyahu once again raised the issue, demanding that Israel maintain a military presence on this border and in the Jordan Rift Valley, based now on the rationale of possible terrorist incursions. It was rumored that Abu Mazen, in the Kerry mediation, was willing to agree only to a 3–5-year presence, and possibly joint Israeli-Palestinian border personnel.

The issue, in the eyes of the Palestinians, is one of sovereignty but, beyond the matter of principle, *de facto* Israeli control over Palestine's eastern border (with Jordan) would mean continued Israeli control over all the land entries and exits to Palestine – a form of continued occupation. This should be kept in mind even in the case of a transition period of 3–5 years, for as long as Palestinians perceive the occupation as continuing, there may be resistance or support for spoilers.

Jerusalem

The city obviously has historic, religious and emotional importance which became more acute when the city was divided by a Jordanian built wall after Jordan lost the Arab areas of West Jerusalem and Israel lost the Jewish area of East Jerusalem (which contains the holy places) in the course of the 1948 war.[14] The symbolic importance of Jerusalem is even greater, signifying the historic link and thus the legitimacy of the creation of Israel in this place. This meaning has been emphasized increasingly since 1967, after the two parts of the city were united during the 1967 war and the municipal borders (of East Jerusalem) expanded to three times their size, incorporating some 28 surrounding villages. Rabin adhered to the official Israeli annexation of East Jerusalem and the

13 At Camp David, Israel's military advisor Yanai said an Israeli presence in the Valley was not essential; Sher admitted that such a presence was primarily for psychological purposes to calm the anxieties of the Israeli public.

14 Under the 1947 Partition Plan Jerusalem was to be a *Corpus Separatum* governed by an international body under the UN. This designated status has remained in international law since that resolution.

declaration of the city as Israel's unified capital (1980 law); Barak was willing to discuss Palestinian sovereignty over limited areas on the outskirts and part of the Old City, but Arafat was generally intransigent on this issue, particularly with regard to the holy sites, namely, the Haram al-Sharif/Temple Mount (and contemptuous of Jewish historic claims). Olmert and Abu Mazen appear to have accepted the Clinton Parameters' proposal that the Arab neighborhoods of the city would be under Palestinian sovereignty, the Jewish neighborhoods under Israeli sovereignty, although Abu Mazen was not willing to agree to Israeli control of the Har Homa neighborhood since it was built after the Oslo Accords. He did, however, agree to the other 13 neighborhoods, despite the fact that they are considered settlements built after 1967 He was criticized for this domestically once this concession was leaked. Since these talks, settlers have moved into a number of the formerly all-Arab neighborhoods (e.g., Sheikh Jarrah), rendering it more difficult to implement an arrangement on the basis of the Clinton Parameters.

As in the Clinton Parameters, the Olmert and Abu Mazen talks avoided according sovereignty over the holy places to either side but, rather, treated the "holy basin" in practical terms, allowing for a trusteeship under Saudi Arabia, Jordan, Israel, Palestine and the US to set procedures and regulations for the area (also assuming the continued running of the Islamic sites by the waqf). The Geneva Initiative spelled out in some detail the administrative, logistic and other measures for the city.

The Jerusalem issue (together with the refugee issue) is often viewed as the most difficult to resolve. However, the Olmert-Abu Mazen talks suggest that this is not necessarily the case. Much depends upon how the proposal is presented – preferably as "sharing" the city rather than "dividing" it, with emphasis on the continued involvement of each side with regard to the holy places (the Holy Basin) plus sovereignty over the ethnically determined neighborhoods.

Refugees

This is an emotionally charged issue on both sides, with approximately four million Palestinian refugees listed on UNRWA roles. Arafat was criticized for ignoring the refugees in the Oslo Accords, whom the PLO claims to represent along with the Palestinians living under Israeli occupation.

For Israel, the refugee issue contains an existential threat: the presumed flooding of Israel with hundreds of thousands, even millions of Arabs, obliterating the Jewish character of the state, placing the Jews in the position of a minority. For this reason, the Palestinian demand for a "right of return" is translated to "they want to push us into the sea." And so, Israel rejects UNGA resolution 194 (of 1949) since the Palestinians refer to it as the legitimation of their "right of return."[15] The PLO, including Arafat, has long understood that no Israeli government would permit a blanket return or even very large numbers. The PLO demand has been, rather, for Israel to recognize the principle of the right to return, or, alternatively, at least to acknowledge Israel's responsibility for the creation of the refugee problem, while numbers of returnees could be negotiated. Abu Mazen has gone further, publicly and repeatedly affirming that there is no intention of altering the character of Israel, and the PLO has accepted the API formula which calls for an "agreed upon" solution to the refugee problem, meaning one that is acceptable to Israel as well, although the API also makes reference to resolution 194 – which is a red flag for Israel. Due to the varied interpretations of the resolution, explicit reference to it must be worked out.

Traditionally Israel has not been willing to admit any responsibility for the refugee issue, but Barak as Prime Minister half apologized when he said that he was sorry for the suffering of the refugees; at the Taba talks the Israelis reportedly agreed to a formula accepting some responsibility. Olmert too may have been willing to allow for Israel to acknowledge its part, leaving the negotiations to deal merely with numbers. Together with Abu Mazen, however, no progress appears to have been made on such numbers, Olmert speaking of 15,000 over 10 years, Abu Mazen spoke to the US about 40,000–60,000 though he was rumored to have spoken also about as many as 150,000 (the latter figure may be the one the PLO actually has in mind). Clinton had sought a solution in a formula of 4 options: refugees remain where they are; go to the Palestinian state; go to a third country; go to Israel. In all cases, the perspective host would determine the numbers, but Clinton also sought to use the term return to their "homeland" which implied the part of Palestine in which the state would be created, hoping that would satisfy those who sought to return to their previous homes in today's Israel. Netanyahu has employed the previously official Israeli position (endorsed by President G.W. Bush) that the refugees could return only to the Palestinian state. For Israel, a solution allowing for somewhere in the area of 40,000 or possibly more refugees to return would have to be cloaked in the form of family reunification, but it would also have to be accompanied by some element of apology or acknowledgement of Israel's past role. Israel may agree to contribute to the costs of refugee resettlement (the track-two "AIX group" has published a study of the presumed costs). Israel is likely to

15 The Israeli Foreign Ministry denies this interpretation of the resolution.

demand that its contribution be offset by estimated losses by Jews who fled Arab countries following the creation of the state of Israel.[16]

Settlements

For Israel, the settlements constitute the greatest problem. Judging from the experience of the Gaza evacuations and the attempts to remove unauthorized "outpost" settlements, the task of moving tens of thousands of settlers into settlement blocs, or back into Israel proper, will be of monumental proportions. There are those who believe it cannot be done, and the settler movement itself more than hints that civil war might ensue. Therefore, the possibility that some settlers might remain in the West Bank under a Palestinian state has been suggested, mainly by peace advocates. Various arrangements have been proposed, but the major problems would appear to be (a) presumed Israeli insistence upon maintaining responsibility for the security of settlers remaining in the West Bank; and (b) the continued hostile nature of those settlers who would seek to remain there (for whom sovereignty over *Eretz Israel* is paramount). Other problems of a legal as well as security and political nature could be expected. It does not appear realistic for any settlers to be allowed to remain, outside the blocs that will be annexed to Israel. Unlike the evacuation from Gaza, Israel and the PA might leave the evacuated facilities for use by the Palestinians for absorption of refugees. The economic costs of evacuation and resettlement have been analyzed by an Israeli NGO, and it may be expected that Israel will request assistance from the US (also for the evacuation of Israeli military facilities in the West Bank, as it did in the case of Sinai). Yet, one may argue that the costs of managing the peace may not be as high as the costs of trying to manage the conflict (occupation).

Other Issues

Water, electricity, environment, economic relations, property issues, movement of labor, tourism and other issues, in addition to the arrangements regarding the core issues, will require Israeli-Palestinian cooperation and, quite likely, US assistance in some form. The Geneva Initiative as well as various think-tanks (in Israel as well as in the US), along with track two meetings, have produced plans or ideas for dealing with many of these issues.

---

16 The issue of compensation for the Jewish refugees from Arab countries, to be part of a peace agreement, has been raised a number of times by Israel. The Palestinians maintain, correctly, that the issue has nothing to do with them, but one may expect it to be brought up, certainly in a regional meeting.

Human Rights

The US cannot and should not dictate the domestic policies of either state, but it can promote certain mechanisms to be included in the final agreement to deal with the protection of human rights. These should include proposals for the creation of educational programs and institutions for such issues as the rights of migrant workers, family reunification, gender equality, freedom of expression and assembly, religious freedom and access to holy places, freedom from religious oppression or oppression of any kind, gun regulation, and so forth.

Reconciliation

The negotiations should include arrangements for people to people activity and projects (particularly educational programs) to promote reconciliation.[17] This may be one of the more difficult but essential issues in the long run. Israel is a tiny country and Palestine will be even smaller. Cooperation at almost every level will be required as the two countries will remain intimately connected. Eventually a confederation may in fact evolve, but until then the many years of hostility and bloodshed must be faced, and their lasting traces reduced, as much as possible and at every level.

Implementation

The written agreement can be implemented step by step, over no more than 3 years, but each side must be convinced of the reality of the final arrangement (end of occupation and the creation of an independent state for the Palestinians; end of conflict and all claims as well as full peace for Israelis). Therefore, the first step should include not merely a freeze on settlement construction but actual evacuation of some settlements as a concrete indication of Israeli intentions.

The compensatory step to mollify Israelis at such an early stage, in response to evacuations, would be the Agreement's clauses that account finally and clearly for full resolution of the refugee issue. Alternatively, explicit Palestinian

17 People to people projects were part of the Oslo Accords, often financed by the US and European countries, and far more successful than most realize. The second Intifada brought the collapse of almost all such ventures, but some have remained, others have sprung up in civil society (especially between former fighters, bereaved families, and young people), with PLO encouragement despite Palestinian NGO injunctions against "normalization."

recognition of Israel as a Jewish state – perhaps in the form of a pronouncement and exchange of letters affirming "the rights of Jewish people to self-determination in its own state and the rights of the Palestinian people to self-determination in its own state, without prejudicing or in any way violating the full rights of other nations in each state" or "Recognition of the State of Israel as the national home of the Jewish people and the State of Palestine as the national home of the Palestinian people, in conjunction with the guarantee of equal rights for all inhabitants of both states."[18]

The nature of the agreement itself, but also the genuine commitment of the leaders of the two sides, their legitimacy and credibility, as well as their ability to deal with spoilers and allay the fears (mistrust) of their respective publics, will all be the most important elements of the implementation process. Nonetheless, there are a number of things that the mediator can, and, in some instances must, do in order to ensure full implementation.

Possibly critical (and missing from the Oslo Accords) is the *immediate* provision of a monitoring mechanism which will include third party monitors and security personnel on the ground, working with both sides. Monitoring may be organized along the lines of the Tenet Plan, for example, with US, Israeli, and Palestinian committees for security, economic affairs, civil arrangements, and more, with touchstones and clear time-tables (Golan 2008: 67). This plan carried a clause that "untoward events" should not be allowed to disrupt the security cooperation – a clause that should be included for the entire period of implementation. The creation of the monitoring mechanisms should be accompanied by the installation of an international force (preferably NATO under US command, as agreed in the Olmert-Abu Mazen talks) on the future Palestine-Jordan border (Jordan River), replacing the IDF occupation force in the Jordan Rift Valley, as speedily as possible.

Once the monitors and international force are in place, assistance (logistic, financial) should be accorded to the evacuation and relocation of settlers, beginning with those from the Jordan Rift Valley. These were originally Labor Party settlers and are considered far less extreme than other settlers outside the settlement blocs; therefore, they may be more easily relocated. It may seem counter-intuitive or even counter-productive to begin with settlers from the sensitive eastern border area, rather than those closer to the green line. Indeed, in the past, Israeli abandonment of responsibility for the security of the eastern border area was to be the very last (if ever) step in a process of withdrawal. However, beginning with the Jordan Rift Valley would not only demonstrate

18 The second formulation is that of Col. (ret.) Shaul Arieli, a member of the Geneva Initiative (*Haaretz*, December 21, 2014).

Israel's sincerity in ending the occupation and its control over Palestinian movement, but it would also allow for the gradual building of the new security regime virtually from the outset.

Normally, US assistance in the training of local security forces would be required, but this task was undertaken during the period of the Olmert-Abu Mazen talks and subsequently continued for some time, with effective Palestinian-Israeli security cooperation even until the present time. In the context of implementation of an agreement, the United States might also assist in the facilitation and supervision of weapons confiscation and gun turn-in programs for civilians, both settlers and Palestinians, (aside from authorized security personnel), under a new weapons registration program.

Beyond these measures, many of the tactics employed earlier, during the negotiations, should be continued, such as involving diaspora figures as go-betweens for the US Administration and Israel as well as the American public and Congress; involving and actively pursuing consultation with Arab states, particularly Saudi Arabia, Egypt and Jordan; producing gestures to each of the protagonists, such as televised appearances or even visits by leaders from the opposing side and from Arab states (to the degree possible). It would be most useful to use regional support from countries such as Saudi Arabia with the aim of removing the conflict from the radicals' toolbox as well as to placate Israeli fears and bolster Palestinian determination. The US should also engage in public appearances in Israel and meet quietly with political elites of both sides, including potential – and actual – spoilers. These should include Hamas, for whom quiet dialogue and American incentives for cooperation may prove fruitful.

Engaging civil society in the effort to win and maintain public support is critical (Hoffman 2015). The US should meet with civil society leaders on both sides, including religious leaders and the media, and, so far as possible, with potential spoilers, in secret meetings if necessary. But the US should also seek to engage the assistance of civil society in actual implementation if possible, but certainly in the selling of the agreement to the public, much the way the YES campaign did for the referendum on the Good Friday Agreement in Northern Ireland (Couto 2001: 227; Sommerville & Kirby 2012: 246; Hancock 2011: 97; Hancock et al. 2010). A referendum or election may be necessary in Israel, though not recommended, in order to gain support, depending upon the strength of opposition within the Knesset at the time (and restrictive legislation that may have been passed in the interim). For the Israeli public, emphasis should be placed on the potential losses if the agreement is not fully implemented, namely a return to the cycle of violence and war that would surely ensue, in addition to international isolation, possibly even sanctions, along with harm to Israeli relations with Washington. It would be wise to present the agreement as "the only real alternative." Importantly, the agreement should not be presented or debated on an issue by issue basis; surveys have consistently demonstrated uncompromising attitudes on both sides when responses are solicited on specific issues, but when a whole agreement with compromises (generally along the lines of the Clinton Parameters) is presented as a package, majority support is gained.[19] These have been consistent findings and should be taken into consideration when trying to "sell" the agreement to the Israeli and Palestinian publics.

Looking towards longer term implementation and results, the US should assist in designing, perhaps also organizing, financing, or participating in (as a third party) reconciliation programs such as people to people projects, joint ventures, dialogues and the like. The US might play a similar role for the protection of human rights.

Finally, the US might facilitate or provide long-term, reduced monitoring and also arbitration for the peace agreement in all its aspects. It might involve the EU countries in such efforts, employing plans devised by the Geneva Initiative and various think tanks for longer-term implementation, some of which include estimates of costs (for refugee resettlement, for example) (AIX 2007), along with proposals for international mechanisms or bodies to assist. US initiatives in the long-term implementation will be part of the guarantees offered for the peace agreement itself. Indeed, American guarantees, along the monitoring mechanism, may be the two most important US contributions to long term success (Walter 1997).

Conclusions

With regard to American mediation and the negotiations themselves, a regional framework under international, but mainly US, sponsorship together with direct involvement of Arab states is highly recommended. The Trump administration appears to favor this framework, as does the present Israeli government. However, the benefits that may accrue to Israel in the form of relations with additional Arab states – something that may come with the regional framework – should not be allowed to avoid a focus on resolution of the Palestinian issue. Whichever framework is chosen, the US should assume an active role;

19 Regular surveys conducted by Khalil Shikaki (Palestinian Research and Survey Center, Ramallah) and Jacob Shamir, Truman Center, Hebrew University and Shikaki with Yehuda Meyer, INSS, January 2014.

the US mediator must be fully authoritative, exhibiting a strong personality and clear US backing, commitment, and determination to achieve the goal of a final peace accord (as distinct from partial or interim agreements).

The US should present its own comprehensive plan on the issues (as highlighted above for each issue). This plan should contain clear objectives with touchstones and a timetable of no more than 3 years for full implementation. The plan should provide for both monitoring and US guarantees to the parties in case of violations, plus the measures listed above as part of the implementation. The end-game should be absolutely clear from the outset – for the Palestinians, end of occupation, with the creation of an independent Palestinian state; for the Israelis, end of the conflict and all claims, along with peaceful relations with the Arab states.

In the negotiations themselves, determination and persistence on the part of the US may be critical. The US should carefully maintain a position of impartiality, assuring both sides of US interest in a fair solution that fully resolves the conflict. Carrots (incentives) and sticks (warnings) should be applied, the latter even to the point of exercising pressure on the stronger party, Israel. The Europeans may be involved regarding incentives (and warnings). The opportunities of the present situation in the region (need for cooperation with Israel) should also be exploited to involve the Arab states politically and economically.

In both the negotiation and implementation stages, the US should try to work with the Jewish diaspora and civil society groups, as well as the Arab states, employing "public diplomacy" to actively promote the agreement. Emphasis should be on the agreement as a whole, as distinct from defending or promoting issues separately. The approach should be that the agreement represents the only alternative – for the parties concerned – to repeated outbreaks of violence and war, continued occupation for the Palestinians and insecurity for Israelis. The most difficult task will be overcoming the mistrust and fears of both sides. To counter these, effective monitoring and especially US guarantees may be critical not only for gaining acceptance of an agreement but for ensuring its implementation and durability.

Resolving this conflict will involve a great effort, both political and economic. Resettlement of refugees and settlers, security arrangements, assistance to the new Palestinian state and compensation or incentives to Israel, will all require large sums for which European and Arab involvement as well as that of various international organizations should be mobilized. Skeptics, and especially spoilers, among the parties to the conflict can disrupt and destroy an agreement. To address or marginalize them, American and regional figures of the highest levels, as well as the protagonists themselves, should be involved in promoting the agreement both within the opposing side, and among the US public (Congress, Jewish diaspora) as well as among Islamic circles and parties, such as Hamas, to the extent possible. Beyond immediate implementation, efforts to create genuine reconciliation and cooperation must be undertaken and assisted.

All that said, negotiations and American mediation under the Trump administration will encounter the same problems and obstacles as past attempts, and it is far from certain that this administration will draw any lessons from past experience in order to deal with them. Of particular difficulty will be the increasingly hardline position of the present Israeli government. Adding to this the sympathy and general esteem with which Trump and his entourage relate to Israel and Netanyahu's government, it seems unlikely that this administration will bring significant pressure on Israel regarding positions rejected by Jerusalem in the past. A middle position, for the sake of ego, could be one in which Trump makes do with a deal that is less than a final peace accord, that is, one that he can present as a significant agreement. This does not, however, appear to be his style. Rather, encountering the old problems and obstacles, Trump may simply abandon the effort altogether rather than suffer failure.

References

AIX Joint Palestinian-Israeli International Economic Working Group (2007). *Economic Dimensions of a Two-state Solution*, May. Accessed at: http://www.bgu.ac.il/~arnona/Fourth%20Stage%20Final.pdf.

Clinton, Bill (2005). *My Life – the Presidential Years*. New York: Vintage Books.

Couto, Richard (2001). "The Third Sector and Civil Society: The Case of the 'Yes' Campaign in Northern Ireland." *Voluntas: International Journal of Voluntary and Nonprofit Organizations* 12, 3.

Ellman, Miriam, Oded Haklai and Hendrik Spruyt (2014). *Democracy and Conflict Resolution*. Syracuse, NY: Syracuse University Press.

FRUS (1975). "Memorandum from the President's Deputy Assistant for National Security (Scowcroft) to the President." March 13, XXVI Arab-Israeli Dispute, Doc.144.

Golan, Galia (2008). *Israel and Palestine: Peace Plans and Proposals from Oslo to Disengagement*. Princeton, NJ: Marcus Weiner Publishers.

Golan, Galia (2014). *Israeli Peacemaking since 1967: Factors behind the Breakthroughs and Failures*. London: Routledge.

Golan, Galia and Gilead Sher, editors (2018 forthcoming). *Non-violent Spoiling in a Violent Conflict: The Case of Israel*. Bloomington, IN: Indiana University Press.

Haklai, Oded (2003). "Linking Ideas and Opportunities in Contentious Politics: The Israeli Non-parliamentary Opposition to the Peace Process." *Canadian Journal of Political Science* 4.

Hancock, Landon (2011). "There is No Alternative: Prospect Theory and the 'Yes' Campaign and Selling the Good Friday Agreement." *Irish Political Studies* 26, 1.

Hancock, Landon, Joshua Weiss, and Glen Duerr (2010). "Prospect Theory and the Framing of the Good Friday Agreement." *Conflict Resolution Quarterly* 28, 2: 183–203.

Herzog, Michael (2011). "Minding the Gaps: Territorial Issues in Israeli-Palestinian Peacemaking." *Policy Focus* 116. Washington, DC: Washington Institute for Near East Policy.

Hirsch-Hoeffler, Sivan, Tamar Saguy and Gilad Hirschberger (2018 forthcoming). "The Psychological Effects of Forced Evacuation: The Case of Jewish Settlers as Future Spoilers," in Galia Golan and Gilead Sher, editors, *Non-violent Spoiling in a Violent Conflict: The Case of Israel.* Bloomington, IN: Indiana University Press.

Hoffman, Evan (2015). "Why are Some Mediations Successful and Others Not?" Accessed at: http://buildingpeaceforum.com/2015/06/why-are-some-mediations-successful-and-others-not/.

Kibrik, Roee and Maya Kornberg (2018 forthcoming). "Leaders as Spoilers," in Galia Golan and Gilead Sher, editors, *Non-violent Spoiling in a Violent Conflict: The Case of Israel.* Bloomington, IN: Indiana University Press.

Kurtzer, Daniel, Scott Lasensky, William Quandt, Steven Spiegel and Shibley Telhami (2013). *The Peace Puzzle: America's Quest for Arab-Israeli Peace.* Ithaca, NY: Cornell University Press.

Newman, Edward and Oliver Richmond, editors (2006). *Challenges to Peacebuilding: Managing Spoilers during Conflict Resolution.* Tokyo: UN University Press.

Palestinian Policy and Survey Research Center (Ramallah) (2015). Palestinian Public Opinion Poll No (55).

Sagie, Uri (2011). *Ha-yad she-kaf'ah* (*The Hand that Froze*). Tel Aviv: Yedioth Sfarim, (in Hebrew).

Seliktar, Ofira (2002). *Divided We Stand.* Westport, CT: Praeger.

Sher, Gilead (2006). *Within Reach: The Israeli-Palestinian Peace Negotiations, 1999–2001.* London: Routledge.

Sommerville, Ian and Shane Kirby (2012). "Public Relations and the Northern Ireland Peace Process: Dissemination, Reconciliation and the Good Friday Agreement Referendum Campaign." *Public Relations Inquiry* 1, 3.

Stedman, Stephen (1997). "Spoiler Problems in Peace Processes." *International Security* 22, 2.

Swisher, Clayton and Ghada Karmi (2011). *The Palestine Papers.* London: Hesperus.

Walter, Barbara (1997). "The Critical Barrier to Civil War Settlement." *International Organization* 51, 3: 335–364.

“Going for Broke” on Palestine

Barry H. Steiner
Department of Political Science, California State University,
1250 Bellflower Boulevard, Long Beach, CA 90840, USA
barry.steiner@csulb.edu

Received 21 February 2016; accepted 30 August 2017

Abstract

This article, a corrective to long-time frustration experienced by the United States in mediating Israel-Palestine differences, argues for American recognition of a Palestinian state to reach a two-state solution. Recognition, though not even-handed, constitutes legitimate mediation, as confronting one or another primary antagonist can be a useful mediation strategy. Though Israel is likely to object to US recognition of Palestine, analysis suggests the objection is not likely to lead to a break in Israel-American relations, which would jeopardize the valued Israel-American alliance. Recognition as a fallback option is recommended for the Trump administration's way forward in mediating the conflict.

Keywords

Israel – Palestine – mediation – United States

The United States has a unique but paradoxical role in the Israel-Palestine conflict. It has long-standing connections to each side's leaders; it provides security assistance to each side; and it interprets and reassures each about the

---

* Barry H. Steiner is Professor Emeritus of Political Science at California State University, specializing in war and peace studies. He has articles on arms racing and arms control, diplomacy and national intelligence estimation. His latest book is *Collective Preventive Diplomacy: A Study of International Conflict Management* (Albany, NY: SUNY Press, 2004). He is completing a study highlighting use of an inductive focused comparison method to generate diplomatic theory.

 | DOI:10.1163/9789004393295_005

intentions of its opponent. Yet it is inordinately frustrated in working toward a comprehensive peace that includes an independent Palestine alongside Israel. The Israeli government and the Palestinian Authority, the primary antagonists with which the US has interacted in a Palestinian peace process, impede American peacemaking efforts by their mistrust of each other and of the US. "Like the optimistic Gulliver, [the United States is] faced by small powers with long memories," writes Miller (2008: 66) about America's Palestine mediation. "Sometimes we succeed. But more often than not we are distracted, hoodwinked, sidetracked, or just plain screwed by small powers who want to befriend and use us at the same time" (see Ross 2004; Golan 2015; Kurtzer & Lasensky 2008; Kurtzer et al. 2013; Shlaim 2001; Quandt 2001; Kurtzer 2012).

Contributing to the frustration is American dependence upon the primary antagonists, both of whom have contributed to deadlock. As Miller (2008: 11) has written, "Regardless of what we wanted, the locals had timetables, agendas, and interests of their own. We could press them, cajole them, even threaten to walk away, but if we wanted to broker agreements, we had to get their cooperation." But the necessary cooperation has not been forthcoming despite repeated American efforts to obtain it.

Of the two primary antagonists, however, Israel has been the more formidable obstacle.[1] There are three reasons for this. First, official American support for a Palestinian state is not reciprocated on the Israeli side. Public American governmental support for a Palestinian state dates from the late 1990s, and Quandt (2005: 35) argued that "[t]he idea of a Palestinian state was no longer particularly controversial."[2] Within the current Israeli government, by contrast, support for a Palestinian state is grudging, conditioned upon resolving many issues in dispute, including borders, security against terrorist violence, the status of Palestinian refugees wishing to return to Israel, and the status

1 This is not to overlook that disunity on the Palestinian side is also a problem. For example, Miller (2012: 149) writes that "The absence of one gun, one authority, and one negotiating position is – on the Palestinian side – the greatest obstacle standing in the way of a successful agreement." However, Hamas leaders rivaling Palestinian Authority negotiators have committed to honoring any agreement with Israel negotiated by the Palestinian Authority as long as its terms would be submitted to a referendum, which the Palestinian Authority has agreed to call (Avishai 2011). The mediation mission of John Kerry, discussed below, was disrupted when an attempt at reconciliation between Hamas and the Palestinian Authority was objected to by the Israeli government (Tepperman 2016: 60). This suggests that Israel is blocking Hamas participation, and not Hamas itself. It is for this reason that the Hamas issue is not considered in this article.

2 Hillary Clinton declared in 1998 that "it will be in the long-term interest of the Middle East for Palestine to be a state" (Horowitz 2014).

of East Jerusalem as a Palestinian capital. Additionally, some Israeli Cabinet officials oppose creation of a Palestinian state.

Second, Israel also resists American Palestine mediation because Palestine's state territory must be taken from area now claimed and occupied by Israel. The late Israeli Prime Minister Yitzchak Rabin alluded to the "zero-sum" character of the territorial issue when he declared that "We give, they get" (Ross 2004: 55).[3] The Palestinian Authority wants the US to extract Palestinian territory from Israel, while the Israeli government, not surprisingly, makes it difficult to gain that extraction. Finally, Israel's superior economic and military strength ensures that Israel will be in a better position without agreement than its Palestinian counterpart will, enabling Israel to more easily resist accommodation.

American officials must anticipate mediation difficulties from these sources of resistance. Miller (2012: 148) notes that for any American plan for comprehensive Israel-Palestine peace, "There is no way you will be able to avoid tension with the Israelis." The current American approach to Palestine's mediation not only invites tension with Israel, but it also makes that tension decisive, for two reasons. First, as we will see, Israel has had, in practice, a veto over American mediation proposals. And second, in pushing for comprehensive peace and a Palestinian state, the US lacks a vital enough concern that would warrant an override of Israeli objections.[4] Israel's resistance thus not only slows the American search for peace, but also deters it insofar as American officials despair overcoming the resistance.

But it might be asked why American mediation should be framed directly in terms of primary antagonist resistance, when intense conflict makes party cajoling and issue haggling inevitable. Why, after all, should mediation on Palestine be so inherently difficult? One answer may be that foreign policy in controversial cases typically involves long odds of success; necessity rather than feasibility drives many policy decisions. A prominent American official experienced in Mideast negotiation is said to have told his staff, "Our job is to take a 10 percent chance of success, try to turn it into a 20 percent chance, and

---

3 A study of a series of mediated African conflicts reveals that in all of them "governments perceived the conflicts in a zero-sum context" (Maundi et al. 2006: 176).

4 American policy officials have debated the importance to the US of Palestine statehood. Miller (2012: 141) maintains that comprehensive Israel-Palestine peace ["Comprehensive Peace"] requires understanding that objective "not just [as] a personal commitment but a vital national interest", but Quandt (1986: 334) contends with respect to American Israel-Palestine peace objectives that "To find a compelling reason for American leadership requires a longer perspective than most American administrations seem to have."

hope for a break" (Roberts 2016). But the problem of long odds should encourage policy planners to develop alternate policy instruments and objectives.

The issue here is not the goals of comprehensive Israel-Palestine peace and a Palestinian state, but rather the most efficient way of pursuing and attaining those objectives. This article takes the viewpoint of an American policy planner looking to enhance Israel-Palestine mediation by maximizing American leverage to push Israel and the Palestinian Authority toward a two-state solution. Because removing the Israeli veto is key to this enhanced American mediation, this article studies how American mediation might proceed toward the two-state objective if Israel no longer had a veto over American peace proposals, and if the US acted to neutralize the impact of Israeli resistance to that objective.

Enhanced mediation is of theoretical interest in the most difficult cases in which repeated settlement efforts do not produce dispute "ripening" – that is, enhanced negotiability of issues in conflict (Zartman 1988; Maundi 2006; Zartman 1995; Touval & Zartman 1985; Bercovitch 1996; Bercovitch & DeRouen 2004; Zartman & deSoto 2011; Steiner 2009; Princen 1992; Beardsley 2011). Considerable attention has been given to mediations in a so-called mutually hurting stalemate (MHS), when each antagonist is strong enough to cause substantial pain to its adversary, and the mutual danger of force escalation enhances mediation leverage. Richard Holbrooke's successful effort to bring an end to the civil war in Bosnia-Herzegovina in 1995 is an example of bolstered mediation with MHS (Holbrooke 1998). The Palestinian case does not feature MHS, however, and as a result, its antagonists absorb and extend long-term stalemate. Enhanced mediation has not, to the present writer's knowledge, been studied in such instances.

The mediation strategy discussed here as the candidate for enhanced mediation, termed "Going for Broke" (GFB), is American recognition of a Palestinian state. The following section introduces this strategy. The sources of present Israel-Palestine deadlock are then addressed, giving special reference to the failure of US Secretary of State John Kerry to bridge Israeli-Palestinian differences in 2013–14, and to how a GFB initiative might have improved Kerry's result. The article then discusses how GFB in the Palestinian case might employ tactics which change conditions of the dispute and introduce new pressures on the antagonists.

The next section launches a policy planning analysis, taking American-Israeli conflict over peacemaking as the key obstacle to GFB success. Using the method of focused comparison, three historical cases are taken as prototypes to three distinct American negotiating strategies to manage American-Israeli conflict: confronting Israel, conceding to it, and postponing the choice

(George 1979). Next, we compare these cases. The option of postponing choice suggests applying the distinction between an ideal "First-Class" mediation solution obtained through cooperation of the primary antagonists, and a fall-back, acceptable "Second-Class" solution in the absence of such cooperation (Stedman 1993: 12; Carrington 1987: 287ff).

We also employ a decision tree to track the variable consequences of GFB. It finds that the "Second-Class" solution is the most likely result, but that Israel's security condition provides the US with adequate enough leverage to ensure that Israel will not interfere militarily with Palestinian state creation. In the conclusion, we offer a short postscript with a preliminary view of the new Trump administration's priorities on Palestine in light of GFB.

Introducing "Going for Broke"

GFB entails American recognition of a Palestinian state and Palestinian independence from Israel. With it, the US would cooperate with the Palestinian Authority for Palestine's state creation, and would no longer need to work for Israeli consent to this development through persuasion or coercion.[5]

The US has important assets to help sustain a Palestinian state despite Israeli opposition. It could capitalize upon long-standing US-Israeli security cooperation, which Israel would presumably wish to continue. It could also continue to assist in reconciling Palestinian security interests with those of Israel. It is difficult to believe that Israel's security can be enhanced without security ties to the US. These arguments suggest that Israel would probably not employ force in response to an American-supported Palestine's declaration of independence, and would limit its opposition to diplomatic action.

Yet even diplomatic Israeli opposition would be difficult for the new Palestinian state and for its American supporter and protector. GFB would probably provoke strong and intense public and Israeli governmental opposition, which in turn would risk not only US-Israel deadlock, but also, if the deadlock were unbridgeable, the ongoing US-Israel alliance. West Bank Jewish settler opposition to GFB and a Palestinian state would be more vocal and intense than at the Israeli governmental level, even if assurances were provided about protecting Jewish settlement blocks. Settler insecurity could contribute to violence between Jewish settlers and Palestinian inhabitants of the West Bank area.

5 Removing the need for coercion responds to Miller's point (2012: 150) that the US can nowadays no longer try to gain Israel-Palestine peace by "Lone Ranger" efforts.

These difficulties must be compared with current American problems in the Israel-Palestine conflict. Miller (2012: 148) writes that "The bottom line with the Israelis is stark and unavoidable. Unless you bring the Israelis around on the importance, advantages, and feasibility of a deal with the Palestinians, you won't even be able to get started." But negative assessments of GFB uncritically assume that future American mediation should be much like the past. The US-Israel security partnership justifies the current American mediating strategy that entails an Israeli veto. It does not necessitate that strategy, however, since allies often act independently, contest each other's policies, and have divergent interests. And when partnership supports a common mediation strategy, it is difficult to understand why mediation should then encourage hard bargaining on peacemaking terms, as the US attempts to overcome objections from the primary antagonists.

Finally, the character of the security partnership may determine the leeway available to the parties to disagree over mediation and peacemaking, before the partnership itself is questioned. If the security partnership is strong, allies may reserve the right to disagree on mediation and peacemaking. If the partnership is weak, differences between them over the value of the partnership could strengthen the bargaining position of the ally least committed to it.

Diagnosing Deadlock over Palestine

American mediation difficulties on Palestine can be explained by: the primary antagonists' hostile and mistrustful political relationship; their acceptance of bearable stalemate; successful American crisis management, which limits the cost and pain of the stalemate; and an American approach that accords the primary antagonists a veto on any mediation proposal. Each of these are reflected in Secretary Kerry's recent mediation efforts.

Hostility and Mistrust

The political relationship between the antagonists has impeded American mediating success over Palestine. The Kerry initiative made considerable progress on security and territorial questions, but the primary barriers to success were said to be outside the negotiations, particularly in the politics surrounding peacemaking negotiations rather than the negotiating issues themselves. "The formal negotiations," a post-mortem analysis concluded, "had always been secondary. They helped define the gaps between the two sides, but they couldn't close them" (Birnbaum & Tibon 2014).

Among the political factors were demands by the parties that reflected a trust deficit. The deficit, produced by prior failures in peacemaking mediation, spread pessimism and cynicism that complicated American efforts to influence the parties. Each side – highly pessimistic about the chances of negotiating success – argued that the opponent needed to make some concession to justify resuming negotiations. The Palestinian Authority demanded release of 104 Palestinians imprisoned by Israel prior to the 1993 Oslo Accords; Israel agreed to release them in four stages over a nine-month negotiating period, but, after reserving the power to decide on the fourth stage later, failed to approve the fourth stage release. Israel demanded adding 2000 units to existing Israeli settlements in the West Bank, which had been opposed by the Palestinian Authority and the US; Kerry reluctantly agreed. Misunderstanding occurred over which homes were included in this demand. The demands, agreed to by the parties through Kerry's insistence – according to one evaluation, "against all odds" – left Kerry the task of building sufficient trust between the antagonists to ensure their implementation (Birnbaum & Tibon 2014: 8). This proved unrealistic, as the window of negotiations was too short to deal with the many issues needing resolution.

Relaxing the requirement of the parties' consent removes the trust deficit as a negotiating problem, and also gives the US more leverage over the antagonists. American ties with the parties contribute to this leverage. Zartman and deSoto (2010: 36) note that:

> Conflicts are ripened when the cost of third-party relations outweighs the potential benefits of the conflict.... [M]ediators serve as crutches or surrogates for trust between the parties, and often their relations with the parties are more important than the cost of the conflict.

Soft Stalemate

Israel-Palestine conflict resists mediation because the antagonists prefer stalemate to a change in the status quo.[6] One basis for this preference is leaders' uncertainty about whether alternatives to stalemate will be publicly supported. Quandt (2005: 19–20) contends that the failure of Israeli-Palestinian negotiations has been mainly due to "the weak domestic base of support of the leaders who were in charge of the negotiations. Time and again, they seem to have hesitated to make moves that might have advanced the negotiations for fear

6 The deadlock is one of many that, as Zartman has written, is "soft stalemate that is stable and self-serving ... with a painful but bearable effect" (2005: 11).

of losing domestic support."[7] Saunders (1991: 159) maintains that mediation efforts must broaden the political base for diplomatic peacemaking. He would include in a peace process "a political period before negotiation – a period of analysis and precipitating a commitment to negotiate – followed by a period of arranging negotiation, negotiation itself, and implementation."[8]

During Kerry's mediation, Israeli Prime Minister Benjamin Netanyahu's control over his Likud party weakened, and Naftali Bennett, the leader of the Jewish Home party in Netanyahu's coalition, was said to be "acting like the coalition partner from hell," interpreting Netanyahu's actions as being contrary to the Prime Minister's values (Birnbaum & Tibon 2014: 13, 16). Yet Kerry lacked time to follow Saunders's advice and broaden Israeli political receptivity to peacemaking; he sought to build upon an overworked set of issues within a non-extendable nine-month negotiating period.

To overcome the antagonists' soft stalemate, GFB could be designed to reorient their perceptions, as Zartman (2005: 12) notes, "out of a general context, with no other justification than the impending catastrophe on the distant horizon." The mediator justifies her intervention by altering the antagonists' objective relationship, removing the status quo as a "comfort zone" (Zartman & deSoto 2010: 33).[9] Past changes in the Mideast status quo have "knocked the parties off balance, changed their calculations, and offered them some potential gains" (Miller 2012: 140). Egyptian President Anwar Sadat's visit to Jerusalem in 1977 emboldened the US to invite Sadat and Israeli Prime Minister Menachem Begin to Camp David in 1978, where the framework for an Israel-Egyptian peace treaty was agreed to. American success in the 1991 Persian Gulf War enabled the US to push the primary antagonists and Arab states to attend the 1991 Madrid Peace Conference, in which Israeli and Palestinian representatives met for the first time. American recognition of a Palestinian state would arguably have comparable impact upon the parties. Even if made conditionally, it would likely surprise the antagonists and affect their calculations and relationship. The mediation challenge would be to capitalize on that effect.

---

7 In an earlier study, Quandt (1986: 22) emphasized the importance of domestic politics for American mediation efforts. Writing about the third year in the presidential term cycle, he noted that "The price of agreement may become very high as the parties to the conflict realize how badly Washington wants a success. Political considerations tend to override the requirements of steady, purposeful diplomacy."

8 Saunders went on to note that the political period includes prenegotiation, by which he meant "all that happens in the political arena before negotiation regardless of what instrument the policymaker eventually chooses for dealing with a problem."

9 Zartman (2005: 11) wrote that in cases of soft stalemate, the mediator's intervention "has to be sold to the conflicting parties themselves (as well as to the intervenors' public)."

American Crisis Management

American crisis intervention, defusing and anticipating cycles of Israeli-Palestinian violence, has helped make peacemaking failures and continuing stalemate tolerable. The delicate character of the Israeli-Palestinian relationship comes from Palestinian frustration with Israeli occupation, combined with the Israeli tendency to assume that its security problems cannot be solved but only managed. "Israel appears trapped in cyclical confrontations," according to one study, "mounting periodic military offensives, but never bringing encounters to anything approaching a discernible outcome" (Puri 2016: 138). Dealing with these cycles, the US has supported Israeli military retaliation to Palestinian terrorism from Gaza in accordance with Israel's war plan and cooperated with Israel to terminate Palestinian use of force (Steiner 2012). But the US has also helped stabilize the relationship by working for security cooperation between Israel and the Palestinian Authority, including strengthening Palestinian policing to dampen demonstrations against Israeli authority in the occupied areas (Tenet 2007: 87ff).

Crisis management between the primary antagonists hampers American peacemaking efforts. Security stabilization enhances the status quo, and therefore does not strengthen diplomatic mediation. Deadlocked yet coexisting antagonists are unlikely to have strong incentives to accept comprehensive peace proposals. Thus, American stabilization efforts may have contributed more to deadlock than to a diplomatic settlement. Furthermore, while the US cannot afford to neglect peacemaking, its peace efforts receive relatively less attention as stabilization efforts receive more. Baker and Berger (2012: xi) worry that

> Arab-Israeli conflict ... will end up diverting the president's attention and absorbing more energy in crisis stabilization than what might have been needed for crisis aversion. We are not prophets of doom and gloom. We are simply looking at realities that have confronted every administration that has tried to wish away its involvement in Arab-Israeli peacemaking.[10]

GFB would assist American peacemaking on Palestine in two ways. First, it would decouple peacemaking from security stabilization initiatives that have narrowed and diminished peacemaking opportunities. Second, GFB, which changes the definition of Israel-Palestine conflict, could employ diplomatic crises for peacemaking purposes. Instead of primarily reacting to the antagonists'

10 Condoleeza Rice (2011: 603) reports that from late 2004, when she became the US Secretary of State, until late 2007, she visited the Middle East twenty times.

security problems, as it has thus far, the US would proactively push for Israel-Palestine comprehensive peace.

The American Mediation Approach

Israel's status as an American ally, and its superior military and political position relative to the Palestinians, assure it special mediation attention. For example, the US has been required to clear its mediation proposals first with Israel before approaching the Palestinian side.[11] "The idea that the United States has consistently been a strictly honest broker adopting positions that are balanced equally between the two sides has always been an illusion," Miller has written (2012: 146). "Israel occupies a place of pride in America's peace process world." This special relationship was reflected during the Kerry mission and criticized by the Palestinians. "[F]rom the beginning [President Mahmoud Abbas] felt as if Kerry was privileging Netanyahu's needs over his.... Kerry had met with Israeli Prime Minister Netanyahu nearly twice as often as with him" (Birnbaum & Tibon 2014: 19).

Miller, an advisor to secretaries of state who has characterized the US as "Israel's lawyer" (2008: 75), argues (2012: 147) that:

> In a high-stakes negotiation, it's ... critical that you not be perceived to be running American ideas by Israel for approval first. This was a serious problem at the second Camp David Summit [in 2000]. We had a no-surprises policy of intimate coordination that resulted essentially in Prime Minister [Ehud] Barak telling President Clinton what he could offer to the Palestinians and what he couldn't. It's one thing for the Israelis to use us to convey their ideas. But when Israel is given a veto power over our thinking and proposals, we can't function credibly.

If Israel can veto American proposals, tensions with the Israelis cannot contribute to agreement, but instead only bring deadlock.

Though politically desirable, neither the veto nor even-handedness is a mediation requirement. GFB, highly favorable to the Palestinians, violates the standard of mediating with even-handedness, but it enhances the mediator's leverage by liberating her from the demands of both sides. As Zartman (1991: 512) notes, a mediator logically has greater difficulty satisfying both primary

11 This was demanded by Israel and evidently conceded by the US in negotiations leading to the 1991 Madrid Conference (Ross 2004: 78).

antagonists than to satisfy one of them.[12] And more importantly, mediation is not confined to *reducing* conflict. "Too often," Bartos and Wehr (2002: 7) note,

> managing, reducing, and resolving conflict has simply deterred or postponed needed changes in power relations. In some cases, conflict management and reduction are the approach most productive of beneficial change; in other cases, it is best to escalate conflict and contest power.

It might be presumed that a mediation orientation that rejects a veto by the primary antagonists and increases conflict with and between them needs to be justified by a US vital interest. However, independent and upgraded diplomatic mediation on Palestine need not be "vital." Instead, such a posture, and the GFB strategy that it pursues, can diminish the prominence of a question that has distracted American policy officials from more important matters, complicated American relations with other powers, and required American diplomats to exert far too much effort upon it.

GFB as Mediation

Intended to spur two-sided negotiations toward a diplomatic objective, GFB responds to mediation problems and strengthens the mediator's leverage in two ways. It reflects: (1) the search for leverage to spur negotiating movement; and (2) the fundamental conflict between the primary antagonists' interests, which hampers the search for a mutually acceptable negotiating formula. We discuss these in turn.

Mediation leverage is usually understood in relation to antagonists who experience mutual pain and heavy costs in an MHS condition, and thereby are attracted to unilateral action to relieve themselves of those pressures (Zartman 2000). The mediator seeks to forestall such action. "[T]he mediator may even need to reinforce a stalemate," write Touval and Zartman (1985: 11), "using its own resources to add negative arguments and inducements to keep the parties from trying to resolve the situation unilaterally." But Israel and the Palestinian Authority are not subject to MHS[13] (Maundi 2006: 162).

---

12 Zartman (1991: 512) also notes that "[H]elpful intervention [by which he means *mutually* helpful] is more difficult by its nature than intervention that supports one side or the other."

13 In later writing, the idea of fostering stalemate between the parties is linked to the absence of ripeness of dispute settlement (Maundi 2006: 162).

In the absence of MHS, an independent-minded American mediator can use GFB to push negotiation movement. We have already noted how the mediator can use her country's relationship between the antagonists, and diplomatic crises, to promote conflict with and between the antagonists to gain such movement. A third source of mediation leverage for movement is diminished asymmetry of Israeli-Palestinian capabilities. Currently, Israel's superior capability in relation to the Palestinian Authority makes it difficult for the US to oppose Israeli officials who reject negotiations and promote a so-called "one state" solution of a Palestinian entity under Israeli authority. American recognition of Palestine adds to Palestine's negotiating leverage, making the antagonists more equal in strength. A fourth source of leverage comes from the possibility of negotiating with a more receptive antagonist separately. If one opponent decides not to participate, ensuing one-sided negotiations can still enhance the security positions of both antagonists. And initiating, or threatening to initiate, separate negotiations may attract the participation of an antagonist that is opposed to negotiations, but decides to participate in a settlement rather than remain outside it.

American mediation techniques must also be adapted to conflicting Israeli-Palestinian interests. The biggest shortcoming in American mediation on Palestine is not the search for shared perceptions or definition of their conflict; neither seems attainable (Raiffa 1982: 215–216). Without shared perceptions, there can also be no transition toward an agreed upon goal (Zartman 1988). The practical negotiating problem is that the antagonists understand Israeli-Palestinian relations very differently and cannot reconcile those understandings. The Israeli government and settlers envision a Palestine deferential and subordinate to Israeli authority, while Palestinian leaders aim for self-determination, with a Palestinian state functioning as an equal to Israel. Under these circumstances, moving the antagonists beyond their current deadlock makes it desirable to build elements of an agreement inductively, irrespective of how those elements are interrelated (Zartman & Berman 1982: 89ff).

Comparing Cases of US-Israel Mediation Conflict

Anticipating Israeli opposition to GFB, American policy planners can usefully compare three possible American choices to US-Israeli conflict: (1) confronting the Israelis; (2) conceding to Israeli views; or (3) postponing this choice, leaving it to depend on the progress of negotiations. The first of these choices tests Israeli reactions to GFB, while the second and the third reject GFB. Each choice corresponds to a historical example in which the US persuaded skeptical

Israeli leaders to negotiate about a Palestinian peace process: (1) American confrontation was successfully employed to bring a reluctant Israeli Prime Minister Yitzchak Shamir to the 1991 Madrid Conference, at which Palestinians were present for the first time; (2) American concession gained agreement between Prime Minister Benjamin Netanyahu and the Palestinian Authority at the 1998 Wye conference; and (3) American postponement of the choice gained agreement between Israeli Prime Minister Menachem Begin and Egyptian President Anwar Sadat at Camp David I.[14]

To highlight barriers from recalcitrant Israeli officials that are erected against American mediators, we ask the following common questions of our three cases: (1) What was the US proposal, and what led the US to choose the option it did? (2) What were the difficulties and limitations of this option? (3) What impact did the option have on Israel? (4) What contributed to American success? and (5) What were the immediate consequences of agreement?

The Madrid Conference

The 1991 Madrid Conference launched a peace process based on dialogue between Arab leaders and Israel, and on the formula of land for peace (Ross 2004; Miller 2008; Kurtzer et al. 2013; Baker 1995). Following the 1991 Gulf War, the American government pledged to address larger Mideast issues, and Secretary of State James Baker (1995: 415) sought a more inclusive approach to the Palestine question, based upon his view that "any new American initiative would fail if it merely resurrected the diplomatic status quo."

Conference diplomacy was exhausting and for Baker a "high-risk undertaking" (Baker 1995: 416). According to Miller (2008: 201),

> Baker was a tour de force operating in an environment where the laws of gravity were heavily weighted toward pulling you and your proposals into a black hole of failure ... Madrid came out of an environment in which the sides had no contact, no trust, no agreed-upon anything. In fact, they were openly hostile and disdainful.

Shamir, mistrusted by Baker, criticized dialogue as vague and open-ended, leading Baker and President George H.W. Bush to believe, in Ross's words

---

14 While our three cases each illustrated Likud-led Cabinets at work, Israeli Labor governments could also be intransigent on negotiations. On the difficult discussions between US Secretary of State Henry Kissinger and the Golda Meir-led government in Israel, see Kissinger (1982: 619ff).

(2004: 64), that Shamir "had been stringing us along." According to one Israeli account, Shamir "was practically dragged to Madrid by President Bush" (Kurtzer et al. 2013: 29). An Israeli unity government fell when its Labor component insisted on a vote to support the proposals, Shamir split with his Likud colleagues and voted against them, and a Labor-sponsored no-confidence vote passed the Israeli Parliament. Returning as Prime Minister, however, Shamir, who received assurances from Baker for attending the conference, was unwilling to appear to the Israeli public as being the "lone holdout" (Ross 2004: 72, 77).

Success at Madrid came from Baker's decision to force the question of the conference, which was unique in that every Arab leader attended. Also, the Gulf War victory enhanced American negotiating leverage; the US, in one appraisal, "took what was available – a political and procedural opening, not a substantive breakthrough – and converted it into a diplomatic success" (Kurtzer et al. 2013: 30).[15] Baker was helped by an inductive diplomatic method, "cobbling together as much as [he] could get the parties to agree on" (Kurtzer et al. 2013: 22–23).

High on symbolism, the conference called for Israelis and Palestinians to begin with transitional issues for Palestinian self-government, and then address permanent status issues such as Jerusalem, borders, and refugees in the third year of the process (Ross 2004: 80). In the implementation stage, the Shamir government fell a second time over Shamir's unwillingness to abide by American demands (as a condition for loan guarantees given to Israel) that Israel publicize the extent of its economic support for West Bank Jewish settlements.

The 1998 Wye Conference

The October 1998 summit conference in Wye, Maryland yielded an interim Israel-Palestinian Authority agreement to redeploy Israeli military forces in the West Bank (increasing territory in so-called "Area C" controlled by the Palestinian Authority 13% beyond the 1995 Oslo II Israel-Palestine agreement) in exchange for Palestinian Authority agreement to enhance Israel's security against terrorist attacks (Miller 2008; Ross 2004; Tenet 2007). Palestinians viewed Israeli redeployment as a move toward permanent Israel-Palestine borders, and desired to limit Israeli security activity in the occupied territory; Israel demanded a security agreement to lessen Palestinian violence against Israel. On the American side, the summit reflected President Bill Clinton's "extraordinary confidence in his own personal skills" (Miller 2008: 277), and the view that American intervention was vital and indispensable "to correct

15 Baker is said to have "made up much of his diplomacy as he went along" (Miller 2008: 201).

the defects of a process that was long since broken and probably beyond repair" (Miller 2008: 269).

Yassir Arafat and Benjamin Netanyahu were very difficult negotiating partners. Clinton "brought two unlikely leaders, filled with mistrust and a fair amount of mutual loathing, together at a summit for the first time" (Miller 2008: 275), and the US became committed to monitor implementation of the Israeli-Palestinian agreement. The Central Intelligence Agency helped develop and implement a Palestinian security plan, particularly against Hamas terrorists from Gaza, that was acceptable to Israel.[16]

Facing resistance in his Cabinet, Netanyahu haggled intensely on the American proposal for a 13% adjustment in "Area C." In grueling negotiations, he highlighted lagging Palestinian action on security procedures, and then insisted on an adjustment whereby 3% of the land would be allocated as a green area, removed from construction and police activity, in which the Palestinians had to coordinate with Israel (Ross 2004: 388ff). He sought to negotiate with the Americans and rely upon them to impose the settlement on the Palestinians (Ross 2004: 394); any viable Israeli proposal had to be sold to the Palestinians as an American one.

Clinton's success came from his belief in working with Netanyahu and not against him. Said to be incapable of "sustained toughness," Clinton became a "Jewish lobby of one" (Miller 2008: 273, 275), while regarding Netanyahu as "a kind of speed bump that would have to be negotiated along the way until a new prime minister came along" (Miller 2008: 273–274). Subsequently, Netanyahu's government broke up over the terms of the agreement, and it was not implemented. "[A] year's work went into oblivion," Miller lamented. "It was a summit about nothing" (Miller 2008: 275).

Camp David Agreement (1978–79)

The 1978 Camp David conference (Camp David I) including President Jimmy Carter, Prime Minister Menachem Begin of Israel and President Anwar Sadat of Egypt, yielded a statement of principles on the West Bank and Gaza and a detailed formula for an Egyptian-Israeli peace treaty providing for full Israeli withdrawal from Sinai bases held since 1967 (Quandt 1986; Miller 2008; Brzezinski 1985; Raiffa 1982).

Following Sadat's trip to Jerusalem early in 1978, the American government committed to making a detailed peace proposal. Carter told his advisors that he intended "to go [for a comprehensive settlement] all the way"

16 Prior Israel-American agreement did not have provisions for American monitoring of security or occupation activities (Miller 2008: 264).

(Brzezinski 1985: 254), and "was gambling that [Israeli Prime Minister Menachem] Begin would prove more flexible once talks were actually under way" (Quandt 1986: 87).

Because Begin and Sadat could not work together, the conference "verged on the edge of complete breakdown almost until the last moment" (Miller 2008: 178–179). Zbigniew Brzezinski (1985: 263), the President's national security advisor, believed that Begin, who favored Palestinian autonomy rather than self-determination, could be "pressured and enticed," and that the President could not afford to fail in his efforts to mediate a settlement. "We must be really ready for a showdown," he wrote to the President. "This means we have to be prepared to think through all of the necessary pressures, including even the ultimate sanction; namely, that refusal to accept our proposals will jeopardize the US-Israeli relationship" (Brzezinski 1985: 251). In July 1978, Brzezinski wrote to Carter that "if we go 'public'" with Israeli rejection of American proposals, "*we must prevail*" (Brzezinski 1985: 250, emphasis in original).

This confrontation strategy was later discarded, because of concerns about the American Jewish community's opposition to American policy (Quandt 1986: 129), because Sadat's trip to Jerusalem "forced Carter to invest in, rather than to confront, Begin" (Miller 2008: 186), and because "Carter long ... understood, apparently better than his advisors had, that no force on earth would drag West Bank concessions from Begin" (Miller 2008: 176).[17] Israel's strategy of holding off concessions on the Sinai until Sadat dropped his demands on the West Bank and Gaza (Quandt 1986: 225), and Carter's conviction that Sadat in practice attached little importance to Palestinian questions, facilitated this retreat (Miller 2008: 173).

Conference success was due, first, to Carter's determination to control negotiation details, while sustaining Sadat's and Begin's engagement (Miller 2008: 176–177); and second, to American willingness to compromise. Had Israel rejected the American-proposed agreement on the Sinai, the administration would have faced media and congressional opposition when explaining that Israel was responsible for the conference breakdown (Brzezinski 1985: 266). Though not linked to the West Bank and Gaza, the Sinai agreement protected Israel from the need to resolve disputes in those areas (Quandt 1986: 256).

A politically risky trip undertaken by Carter in March 1979 to Cairo and Jerusalem to rapidly conclude a treaty based on Camp David successes was received coolly in Jerusalem, in the aftermath of what was termed the "firestorm" reception in Israel of the Camp David agreement (Quandt 1986: 303). Only

17 Quandt (1986: 323) argues that Carter arrived at this position only during the Camp David talks.

when Carter threatened to leave Jerusalem did the Israeli government work to rapidly finalize a treaty. Begin subsequently minimized Palestinian autonomy, and his decision to end a freeze on settlement-building after three months was contrary to what Carter understood had been agreed to at Camp David.

Case Analysis

Israeli leaders in each case parried demands by the US for compromise, and their opposition required interminable American counter-effort. Shamir was asked to make mostly symbolic accommodation. Begin was asked to concede authoritative governmental functions to the Palestinians, going beyond the demand for autonomy. Netanyahu was pressured to give up territory controlled by Israel to the Palestinian Authority. Netanyahu's concessions were neutralized when his government fell, while Begin, whose government was weakened by his concessions on the Sinai, made no concessions on Palestinian governance.

A second case commonality was the special American relationship with Israel, which, along with American attention to the Israeli objections, impaired American ability to push new and innovative mediation steps. The cases suggest that protecting this relationship had higher American priority than peacemaking over Palestine. It provided a safety net that absorbed frictions between the two countries which emerged over peacemaking. Yet while it encouraged a strain on peacemaking agreement, it also appeared to license strong *dis*agreement, and the assumption by Israeli officials, whose security interests in the negotiations were stronger than that of the Americans, that, in Miller's words (2008: 274), "they could push America around and get away with it."[18]

What can be said about the difference between Madrid, when the US confronted the Israelis, and Wye and Camp David I, when it did not? In the former, the tougher American approach seemed to coincide with a decline in Israeli resistance to pressure. American demands to Israel to recognize PLO-sympathetic Palestinians then caused a split in the Israeli national unity government, the Labor contingent being willing to break up the Cabinet for the sake of moving ahead on peacemaking. And Shamir, divided earlier from his own party by his resistance to holding a conference, became more accommodating when he faced the prospect of isolation within Israel over his opposition to negotiations.

The American non-confrontational approach to Camp David I and Wye eased the Israeli negotiation problem by suggesting the US wanted to avoid

---

18 Israel relied on divided American government for this objective (Miller 2008: 148).

a negotiation breakdown. Non-confrontational American officials would not intend – as Baker had done earlier with Shamir – to weaken Begin and Netanyahu at home and/or capitalize on splits within the Israeli Cabinet. A confrontational American approach advocated within the American government in those cases would have necessitated capitalizing upon Begin and Netanyahu's domestic weaknesses (Friedman 1994).

For confrontation-minded American officials, our cases distinguish three ways to capitalize upon Israeli leader weaknesses. One approach, reflected in the background to the Madrid Conference, would accentuate differences on the peacemaking front within Israel by encouraging establishment of a national unity government in which a peace faction would have considerable prominence. The second confrontational approach, contemplated by some of Carter's advisors, would condition the American-Israeli alliance upon Israel cooperation on Palestine. It would be based on the American assumption that Israel values the alliance more than it opposes comprehensive peace. A third approach, postponing confrontation, is suggested by Carter's Camp David I decision not to pressure Begin to make concessions to the Palestinians. Confronting Israel directly was then merely an option that the US ultimately decided not to pursue.

Distinguishing "First-Class" and "Second-Class" Palestinian State Solutions

GFB does not require the US to confront Israel directly. Instead of seeking to force Israel's approval of a Palestinian state, the US would act to protect the Palestinian state against Israeli governmental and non-governmental challenges. This is the most immediate way in which the US can assist the new Palestinian state. The US would seek security cooperation between Israel and Palestine based on the idea that a security threat to either is a threat to both. Its goal would be to establish conditions in which the Palestinian state does not constitute a security threat to Israel, thereby removing one major obstacle to the establishment of Palestine.

Pursuing Palestinian independence from Israel, the US would work over a period of months to facilitate Israeli military withdrawal from West Bank territory (excluding present Jewish settlement blocks) within one year's time.[19] Palestinian police would be charged with maintaining security within the new

19 Avishai (2011) indicates that in their extended discussions in 2008, Olmert and Abbas agreed on all territorial questions except the status of the settlement of Ariel. The

state; Israeli sweeps into Palestinian territory seeking terrorist suspects would be discontinued, and Israeli armed forces would be confined to their bases. Israel would be invited to increase Israeli-Palestinian police and intelligence linkages. Foreign force contingents would replace Israeli ones, and Israel would be asked to gradually release a significant portion of Palestinians in Israeli jails, conditional upon an avoidance of Palestinian-initiated violence.

GFB would operate as two-track policy. On one track, aimed at a comprehensive settlement of Israeli-Palestinian differences, the US would work to have all neighboring states, including Israel, recognize a Palestinian state. This "first-class" solution yields the strongest basis for establishing Palestine.[20] It reduces the likelihood of governmental spoiler activity and ensures that diplomatic relationships will not be ruptured over the creation of a Palestinian state.[21] But this track burdens the mediator with: (1) a wider set of issues injected by Israel and Palestine, and the possibility of hard bargaining over them; and (2) providing considerable incentives and reassurances for countries to participate. Further, Israel may not wish to participate.

Less ambitiously, the US would commit to oppose governmental and/or non-governmental opponents of the Palestinian state, including those from Israel. Opposition to the state would be managed primarily by peaceful diplomatic means, but would entail small-scale American military contingents for defense and deterrent purposes should Israel (in the very unlikely scenario) resist the Palestinian state with force or be unable to control Jewish settler groups that initiate violence. This "second-class solution" settles for less than the ideal in the belief that it is acceptable and sustainable even without the participation of the objecting party.

On the one hand, "second-class" GFB is vulnerable to Israeli spoiler activity, though this is not inevitable from Israel's opposition to a Palestinian state. On the other hand, the "second-class" solution assists the mediator in two ways. First, it reduces the scope of negotiation. Second, by maintaining diplomatic urgency and altering the relationship between the antagonists, the "second-class" approach creates a situation that the primary antagonists will not have anticipated, creating, in Miller's terms (2012: 141), "the disincentives and incentives that give [the parties] a stake." If Israeli leaders should conclude, contrary

---

disposition of settlements could be settled through three-party negotiations or through arbitration.

20 Recognition of Israel by neighboring states that have not yet offered it would also be sought.

21 It does not guarantee this result because a participant can use negotiation for spoiler purposes.

to their present government, that a Palestinian state is viable and/or is preferable to the current deadlock, they may come to accept incentives associated with the "first-class" solution – most notably, being able to influence the contours of Palestine by cooperating to establish it from the beginning rather than by resisting it. For this reason, first-class and second-class solutions, although distinct, are not mutually exclusive. Each is a necessary part of GFB.

Moving beyond History

Israeli reactions to GFB call for American responses in the form of support (tacit or explicit) or of overcoming opposition.[22] Of major concern to the US and Israel in this context is insulating the US-Israel alliance from that opposition.

A decision tree method can clarify inter-relationships between these moves (Starkey 2010: 120–123). American recognition of a Palestinian state would create a decision point for Israel, whose right-wing government would either hold steady or change its orientation, either through formation of a national unity regime or through elections. If the government holds steady, no Israeli willingness to negotiate on the terms of Palestine's independence should be anticipated, given the government's prior opposition to GFB; Israel is more likely to agree to negotiate if the government is altered. The following discussion is limited to the consequences of these two choices.

Change of Israeli Government

If an Israeli national unity government emerges, its next decision point will be to determine whether to negotiate with the Palestinian state and the US about a Palestinian state, based upon determination to retain the US as a close ally. If Israel agrees to negotiate, it would participate in a "first-class" solution of the Palestine issue, while using its willingness to negotiate as leverage to exact considerable demands over the character of the Palestinian state. With its spectrum of interests (possibly including pro-settler representatives) this government's negotiating positions are likely to be highly circumscribed. It might wish to extend negotiations over a long period and haggle over details. Alternatively, the government might be unable to bargain over Palestine, and therefore permit a "second-class" solution, negotiating separately with the US over its terms. Both options presume that Israel would continue to endorse

22 Such analysis can use the rational actor perspective, in which the policy analyst, according to Allison (1971: 35), "puts himself in the place of the nation or government," to identify options and problems that must be alleviated or accepted as manageable.

Oslo agreed-upon provisions for security cooperation with the Palestinian Authority and recognition of that entity.

A second possibility is that a national unity government cannot be formed, perhaps because Israeli advocates of negotiation (including Labor and other centrist parties) cannot establish a common front with pro-settler parties that oppose negotiation, or perhaps because elections are held in which right-wing Israeli parties continue to prevail. Such a government would be unable to participate in a "first-class" Palestine solution and would stand aside from Palestinian state creation, while presumably agreeing not to use force against it.

The next decision point for such a government would be to determine whether Oslo security provisions would remain in effect. A new Israeli government would likely attach considerable importance to retaining the US-Israel alliance, and therefore take security decisions insulating the alliance from GFB effects. Retaining support for Oslo provisions would be one way to provide such insulation by enhancing stability and strength of the Palestinian state and easing American requirements to protect it. Removing support for the provisions would place a much heavier burden on a Palestinian state and its American backers, legitimizing Jewish settler opposition and its resistance to Palestinian state creation. If the Oslo provisions lapsed, and settler-caused violence occurred, the absence of an Israel-Palestine crisis management regime would threaten the spirit of the US-Israel alliance. American officials valuing the alliance would then need to determine whether the weakening of the alliance is an unacceptable GFB cost.

No Change in Israeli Government

A right-wing Israeli government retaining power would be unlikely to negotiate over the terms of Palestine's creation or insulate the US-Israel alliance from GFB effects. It would justify itself with nationalistic rhetoric, outwardly opposing and undermining GFB and, beyond that, highlight policy differences with its American ally. Maintaining that preserving a "greater Israel" is a higher priority than the American alliance, the government would argue that only Israel itself can provide security guarantees against terrorism from the occupied territories; American security assurances fall short because the reasoning behind Israel's need to control the territories extends beyond just security concerns. However, Israel is not likely to immediately repudiate the alliance, given its heavy military and diplomatic dependence on American support.

Such a government would also need to determine whether it will uphold the Oslo security framework. If it does, it will then need to determine whether to upgrade or make overt its current covert support of Jewish settlers opposed to a Palestinian state, and/or authorize the Israeli Army to oppose settler

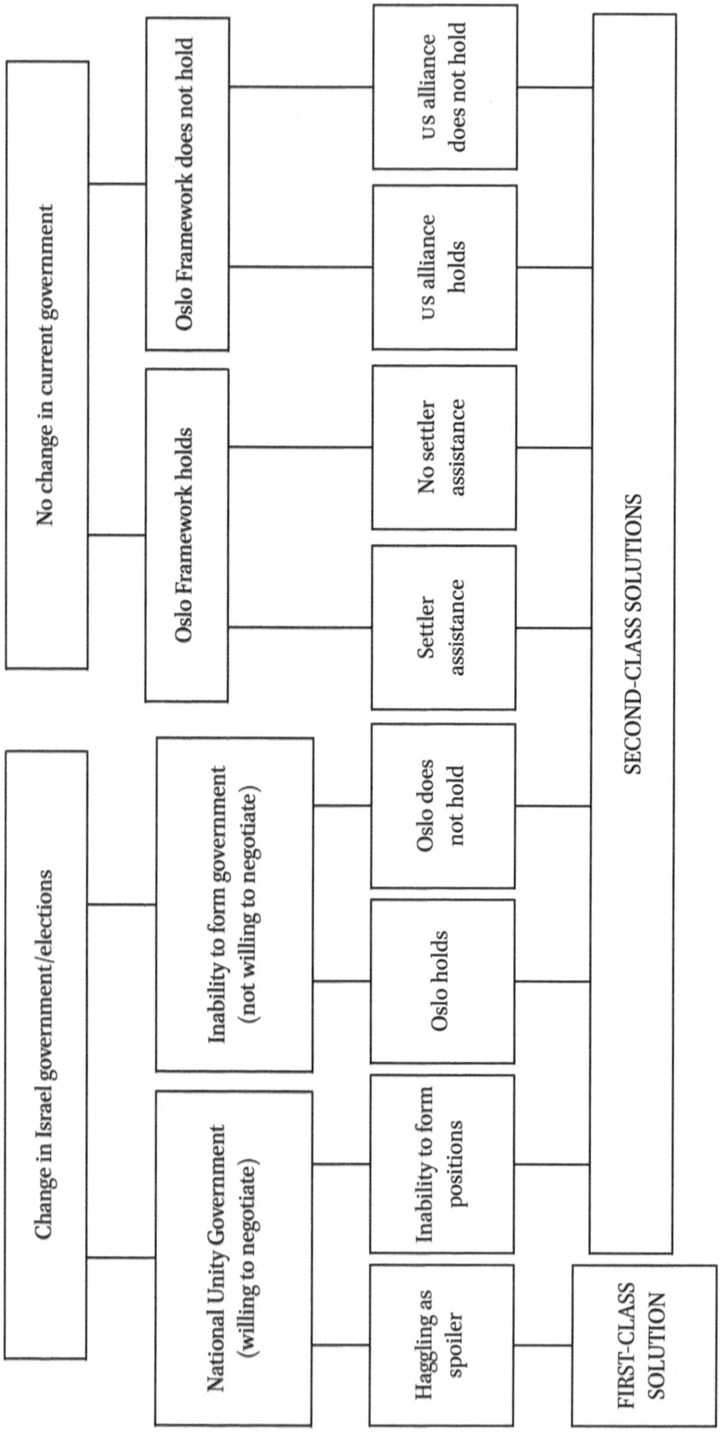

FIGURE 1 Consequences in Israel of US recognition of Palestine

hit-and-run spoiler tactics. Overt assistance to the settlers would seriously threaten the Palestinian state and, because of American assistance to the state, imperil the US-Israel alliance. If retaining the alliance remained an American priority, yet the threat of settler resistance is perceived by the US as threatening the alliance, GFB would be discouraged. Alternatively, the US might not allow the settlers, supported by the Israeli government, a veto over Palestine's creation, leaving it to the Israelis to determine whether the alliance survives.

If Israel repudiates the Oslo framework, its control of the occupied territories would then depend on Israeli military and settler action, despite American opposition. It is hard to envision Israel being more secure in this scenario than at present, and its overt clash with the Palestinian state and with Palestine's American protector would make sustaining the alliance with the US very difficult or impossible. These pathways are summarized above in Fig. 1.

Conclusions

Big powers usually prevail in conflicts with smaller ones, but the frustrating American experience with Israel-Palestine mediation is an exception. This essay argues for outright GFB to bolster American mediation effectiveness in this instance. GFB is not even-handed; rather, it fits into the broader mediation toolkit as a strategy that would *increase* tensions between mediator and primary antagonists to enhance the mediator's leverage.[23] As between the primary antagonists themselves, GFB would narrow the current asymmetry between Israeli and Palestinian capabilities, bolstering the sustainability of a Palestinian state. A more equal Israeli-Palestinian relationship should increase mutual dependence and increase Israeli incentives to accept Palestine as a state.

Israeli governmental and Jewish settler opposition to this strategy must be expected. Taking that opposition as a starting point, this essay has used a policy planning approach to track its form and impact. Eight pathways flowing from GFB have been distinguished, of which only one would bring Israeli acceptance of a "first-class" comprehensive Palestinian settlement, and seven would entail a "second-class" Palestine result without Israeli participation.

Perhaps the best indicator of Israeli government intentions toward GFB and the alliance would be its attitude toward the US-supported Oslo security framework. Support for that framework would mean that Israel-Palestine

23 I am indebted to Professor Zartman for his incisive analyses of a broad variety of mediation initiatives.

collaboration would continue under American auspices, even after "second-class" creation of a Palestinian state. Its rejection would endanger Israeli security as well as the US-Israeli alliance. The essay argues that rejection of that link, and widespread Israeli government and/or Jewish settler activity undermining Palestine's security and welfare, would likely be contained by the vital importance attached to the US-Israel alliance by the US and Israel. This large alliance value provides leverage for the US, a "security supplier," over Israel, a "security consumer," when retention of the alliance link is at issue.[24] Based on this argument, the essay concludes that GFB and Palestinian state-creation can be sustained without Israeli cooperation.

Postscript: The Trump Administration

Mediation proposals and predictions depend upon the mediator's needs as well as those of the disputants. This essay was prepared to provide the Barack Obama administration with the most compelling alternative to Palestinian mediation deadlock. It assumed that President Obama would be receptive to new steps toward Israel-Palestine peace, and that the President and his administration were strongly motivated to escape the deadlock. The analysis was undeterred by the prospect of political fallout at home if Israel opposed American action to break the deadlock; it was believed the administration could sidestep that fallout by breaking the deadlock at the end of an Obama term, much as earlier American recognition of the Palestine Liberation Organization had been done at the end of the presidential term of President Ronald Reagan (Shultz 1993: 1040ff).

The GFB outright strategy described here responds to this challenge, but that strategy must be reconsidered in the context of a Donald Trump administration in Washington. A different GFB scenario accords with President Trump's outlooks, as they are presently understood.

President Trump shares with his predecessor a distaste for prolonged diplomatic haggling, such as would occur on detailed issue-based peacemaking. But the differences in the two leaders' mediation orientations are quite large. Trump is more sensitive to Israeli ambivalence about a Palestinian state, and more inclined to favor Israeli over Palestinian needs, in accord with the Israel-America alliance, than Obama was. Since he is strongly wedded to Israel as an ally, Israeli opposition to GFB would weigh more heavily upon him than

24 The distinction between "security consumer" and "security supplier" was first made by Alastair Buchan in connection to the NATO alliance.

upon Obama, and he is not likely to support GFB without first providing some equivalent or larger benefit to Israel.

President Trump cannot therefore be expected to support GFB outright, but he might well support GFB as a fallback first-step, low-effort alternative to tackling peacemaking details.[25] That is, GFB would be attractive for Trump not for its intrinsic value but because an informal, preliminary negotiating process highlights it as a useful indication of progress. If adequately prepared, this process could neutralize expected Israeli opposition to GFB by increasing American leverage upon the antagonists. It would also give President Trump a central diplomatic role commensurate with his celebrity status.

As envisioned here, GFB would become one element in a triangular negotiation in which the two primary antagonists, each needing American support, compete for it. The US would create such a process by indicating confidentially to both sides that it contemplates Palestinian recognition, and following up to provide incentives to both sides to accept that initiative. To obtain Israel approval of such recognition, or at least the assurance of not impeding creation of a Palestinian state, the US would offer its own security assurances to reduce Israeli anxieties about the dangers of creating a Palestinian state (whose forces would be limited to police, as previously agreed upon). With the Palestinian Authority, the US would develop an agreed time-line for Palestine's state creation, hoping for Israeli support but envisioning a Palestine Unilateral Declaration of Independence in the absence of such support. The US would help create a mechanism whereby the Israeli Army would be removed from the occupied territories and replaced by Palestinian security police, and it would assist as needed in Palestine's economic development.

References

Allison, Graham (1971). *Essence of Decision: Explaining the Cuban Missile Crisis.* Boston, MA: Little Brown.

Avishai, Bernard (2011). "A Separate Peace." *The New York Times Magazine*, February 13.

Baker III, James A. (1995). *The Politics of Diplomacy.* New York: G.P. Putnam's.

25 Although the Palestinian position is, as the writer understands it, that detailed issues such as territorial boundaries, refugees, and the status of Jerusalem must be decided before Palestinian state-creation, that was not Israel's experience when it was created in 1948. "In international law, a state, to be recognized as such, is supposed to have clearly defined boundaries. This was not the case with Israel, or so, at least, it could be argued" (Eytan 1958: 14).

Baker III, J. A. and S. Berger (2012). "Foreword," in Daniel C. Kurtzer, editor, *Pathways to Peace*. New York: Palgrave Macmillan.

Bartos, O. J. and P. Wehr (2002). *Using Conflict Theory*. Cambridge: Cambridge University Press.

Beardsley, Kyle (2011). *The Mediation Dilemma*. Ithaca, NY: Cornell University Press.

Bercovitch, Jacob, editor (1996). *Resolving International Conflicts: The Theory and Practice of Mediation*. Boulder, CO: Lynne Rienner.

Bercovitch, J. and K. DeRouen, Jr. (2004). "Mediation in Internationalized Ethnic Conflicts: Assessing the Determinants of a Successful Process." *Armed Forces & Society* 30, 2: 147–170.

Birnbaum, B. and A. Tibon (2014). "The Explosive, Inside Story of How John Kerry Built an Israel-Palestine Peace Plan – and Watched it Crumble." *New Republic*, July 20. Accessed at: www.newrepublic/com/article/11875/how-israel-palestine.

Brzezinski, Zbigniew (1985). *Power and Principle*. New York: Farrar, Straus & Giroux.

Carrington, Peter Lord (1987). *Reflecting on Things Past*. New York: Harper & Row.

Eytan, Walter (1958). *The First Ten Years*. New York: Simon & Schuster.

Friedman, Thomas L. (1994). "Diplomacy is Minding Other Nations' Business." *The New York Times*, January 30.

George, Alexander L. (1979). "Case Studies and Theory Development: The Method of Structured, Focused Comparison," in Paul Gorden Lauren, editor, *Diplomacy: New Approaches in History, Theory, and Policy*. New York: Free Press.

Golan, Galia (2015). *Israeli Peacemaking Since 1967*. London: Routledge.

Holbrooke, Richard (1998). *To End a War: From Sarajevo to Dayton – and Beyond*. New York: Random House.

Horowitz, Jason (2014). "In Exile." *The New York Times Magazine*, December 21.

Kissinger, Henry (1982). *Years of Upheaval*. Boston, MA: Little Brown.

Kurtzer, Daniel C., editor. (2012). *Pathways to Peace*. New York: Palgrave Macmillan.

Kurtzer, D. C. and S. B. Lasensky (2008). *Negotiating Arab-Israeli Peace*. Washington, DC: United States Institute of Peace Press.

Kurtzer, Daniel C. et al. (2013). *The Peace Puzzle: America's Quest for Arab-Israeli Peace, 1989–2011*. Ithaca, NY: Cornell University Press.

Maundi, Mohammed et al. (2006). *Getting In*. Washington, DC: United States Institute of Peace Press.

Miller, Aaron David (2008). *The Much Too Promised Land*. New York: Bantam Books.

Miller, Aaron David (2012). "Memorandum to the President: Thinking Through an Israel-Palestinian Initiative," in Daniel C. Kurtzer, editor, *Pathways to Peace*. New York: Palgrave Macmillan.

Princen, Thomas (1992). *Intermediaries in International Conflict*. Princeton, NJ: Princeton University Press.

Puri, Samir (2016). "Fighting and Negotiating with Armed Groups." *Adelphi Paper* 2016, no. 459. London: International Institute for Strategic Studies.

Quandt, William B. (1986). *Camp David.* Washington, DC: Brookings Institution.

Quandt, William B. (2001). *Peace Process*, rev. ed. Washington, DC: Brookings Institution.

Quandt, William B. (2005). "Israeli-Palestinian Peace Talks: From Oslo to Camp David II," in Tamara Coffman Wittes, editor, *How Israelis and Palestinians Negotiate.* Washington, DC: US Institute of Peace Press.

Raiffa, Howard (1982). *The Art and Science of Negotiation.* Cambridge, MA: Belknap Press.

Rice, Condoleeza (2011). *No Higher Honor: A Memoir of My Years in Washington.* New York: Crown.

Roberts, Sam (2016). "Harold H. Saunders, 85, Mideast Peace Broker, Dies." *The New York Times*, March 9.

Ross, Dennis (2004). *The Missing Peace.* New York: Farrar, Straus & Giroux.

Saunders, Harold H. (1991). *The Other Walls*, rev. ed. Princeton, NJ: Princeton University Press.

Schelling, Thomas C. (1966). *Arms and Influence.* New Haven, CT: Yale University Press.

Shlaim, Avi (2001). *The Iron Wall.* New York: Norton.

Shultz, George P. (1993). *Turmoil and Triumph.* New York: Charles Scribner's Sons.

Starkey, Brigid, et al. (2010). *International Negotiation in a Complex World*, 3rd ed. Lanham, MD: Rowman & Littlefield.

Stedman, Stephen J. (1993). *The Lancaster House Constitutional Conference on Rhodesia.* Pew Case Study in International Affairs #341. Washington, DC: Institute for the Study of Diplomacy, Georgetown University.

Steiner, Barry H. (2009). "Diplomatic Mediation as an Independent Variable." *International Negotiation* 14, 1: 7–40.

Steiner, Barry H. (2012). "What Use Overwhelming Air Superiority? A Tale of Two Campaigns." *Contemporary Security Policy* 33, 2: 311–336.

Tenet, George (2007). *At the Center of the Storm.* New York: HarperCollins.

Tepperman, John (2016). "A Conversation with John Kerry." *Foreign Affairs* 95, November/December.

Touval, S. and I. W. Zartman, editors. (1985). *International Mediation in Theory and Practice.* Boulder, CO: Westview Press.

Zartman, I. William (1988). "Alternative Attempts at Crisis Management: Concepts and Processes," in Gilbert Winham, editor, *New Issues in International Crisis Management.* Boulder, CO: Westview.

Zartman, I. William (1991). "Negotiations and Prenegotiations in Ethnic Conflict: The Beginning, The Middle, and the Ends," in Joseph V. Montville, editor, *Conflict and Peacemaking in Multiethnic Societies.* New York: Lexington.

Zartman, I. William (ed.) (1995). *Elusive Peace: Negotiating an End to Civil Wars*. Washington, DC: Brookings Institution.

Zartman, I. William (2000). "Ripeness: The Hurting Stalemate and Beyond," in P. C. Stern and D. Druckman, editors, *International Conflict Resolution after the Cold War*. Washington, DC: National Academy Press.

Zartman, I. William (2005). *Cowardly Lions*. Boulder, CO: Lynne Rienner.

Zartman, I. W. and M. R. Berman (1982). *The Practical Negotiator*. New Haven, CT: Yale University Press.

Zartman, I. W. and A. deSoto (2010). *Timing Mediation Initiatives*. Washington, DC: United States Institute of Peace Press.

Beyond Exacerbating Asymmetry and Sustaining Occupation: An Alternative Approach for United States Intervention in the Israeli-Palestinian Conflict

Walid Salem
The Center for Democracy and Community Development – East Jerusalem, P.O. Box 20510 (Salah Eddin Street Post Office), East Jerusalem-Via Israel
walidsociety@gmail.com

Received 21 February 2016; accepted 11 August 2017

Abstract

Third party mediation is critical in pushing forward a new peace process that is based on Israeli and Palestinian compliance in fulfilling previous agreements, including an Israeli freeze on settlements. The freeze will be part of a transformative constructionist process that will allow both sides to negotiate from a more symmetrical position. It will also create more trust among the Palestinians by communicating that Israeli intentions are not about grabbing their land while discussing peace.

Keywords

United States – Israel – Palestine – mediation – conflict transformation – constructionist approach

* Walid Salem is a doctoral candidate in International Relations at Near East University and a lecturer on democracy, human rights and conflict resolution at Al Quds University. He is an author of more than thirty books and many articles on issues of democracy, citizenship, non-state actors and civil society, peacebuilding, narratives, conflict resolution, and Islamic movements. He is the Director of the Center of Democracy and Community Development in East Jerusalem.

 | DOI:10.1163/9789004393295_006

This study suggests a new approach to American mediation in the Israeli-Palestinian conflict. It argues that this approach would bring about an end to the 1967 Israeli occupation of the West Bank, Gaza Strip, and East Jerusalem in order to create a viable, independent, contiguous, and democratic State of Palestine that lives in peace and security beside the State of Israel. It would serve as a point of departure for dealing with these territories as areas that are under dispute, recognizing that both sides have equal claims toward them as a whole or in part, as in the case of East Jerusalem and Area C. The article begins with a summary of the results of American mediation over the last 25 years, followed by a brief review of the path of Israeli-Palestinian negotiations, and the role of American mediation.

An alternative approach for American mediation is discussed, which I shall term the "constructionist approach" to transform the conflict toward a two-state solution. This approach is ethically based and includes a combination of peacemaking (i.e. for example, negotiation), peacekeeping (for example the allocation of international forces), and peacebuilding by creating Palestinian facts on the ground to reach a more symmetrical position with Israel when negotiating. Within the framework of this constructionist approach, the short and long-term actions for the political track are presented first, followed by the required actions needed for the economic and security tracks. When discussing these tracks, the roles of different local, regional and international actors will be included with an emphasis given to the role of the United States in generating the joint Israeli-Palestinian efforts.

This article is by no means an exhaustive overview of American policy toward the Israeli-Palestinian conflict – a vast body of literature presently exists addressing this topic (Gerges 2013; Aruri 2012; Chomsky 1999). Nor is it a review of the internal Israeli and Palestinian political structures, contradictions, rifts, and their influence on the American mediation process. The article also does not concern itself with the roles of Jewish and Arab lobbies in influencing US policy, relations between the White House and Congress, or US decision-making processes. The status of Israeli-American or Palestinian-American relations, their past and future developments and the efficacy of American mediation are not examined. In this study, it is argued that the United States can be more than a mediator in the conflict, and that it can play the role of arbitrator, doing more for peacebuilding by assisting to establish a State of Palestine beside the State of Israel. It is argued that this can only happen if the United States abandons the realm of realism that prioritizes Israeli interests over Palestinian interests, enhancing Israeli power in the conflict. Alternatively, if America were to assume an ethically grounded approach, based on inclusion of both parties, there would be a fair distribution of justice.

An Objective Outcome of American Mediation: Sustaining Occupation via Negotiations

Since the Madrid Peace Conference of October 1991, the last 24 years of the Palestinian-Israeli negotiations have, despite the good intentions of third party interveners, resulted in a deepening of the Israeli occupation. This has caused asymmetry of negotiating status, asymmetry of power (Heller & Nusseibeh 1991: 30), asymmetry of regional and international status, and asymmetry on the ground. Taken together, these effects have exacerbated the asymmetry of the conflict as a whole, rather than narrowing it toward a solution (Kahanoff, Salem, Nasrallah & Neumann 2007: 33, 109, 130, 143; Grinberg 2007: 571–572).

The approach to negotiations has been inadequate and process-driven, prioritizing, at each stage, the compromises required to bring the two sides to the negotiation table. This pattern was exemplified by George Mitchell in 2010 and again by John Kerry in 2013. In each instance, the intervener initiated a process that created different and contradictory expectations about results in the minds of the antagonist parties, rather than focusing on a peace process (Erekat 2010a; 2010b; 2010c; 2013).

Further, when the "end of conflict" deal was discussed in negotiations at Camp David in 2000, it centered on how to divide the 1967 occupied Palestinian territories between the two sides. This would lead to a greater Israel and a decreasing Palestine, rather than constructing a pathway toward a historical compromise between the two-states with an agreed solution to the Palestinian refugee problem (Chomsky 1999; Said 2001).

The compromise process since Madrid in 1991 was based on the concept of considering the Palestinian territories, occupied in 1967, as an area under dispute. The fate of the territories was to be decided within an open-ended process at a later date (Gazit, Shehadeh & Abdel Shafi 1994), and therefore subject to bargaining between the two sides. The result was that all territorial Palestinian rights based on the 1967 borders became disputable. The significance of the Oslo compromise, which was about Palestinian recognition of Israel in 78 percent of Palestine drawn from 1948 borders, is taken at the expense of the Palestinians who would only get the other 22 percent of land occupied in 1967. This 22 percent became the subject of competition in dividing the territory between the two sides. This process will lead to the establishment of a Palestinian Authority without authority and an occupation without cost. It keeps Gaza outside the Palestinian space, changes the situation on Al-Haram Al-Sharif, allows for continuation of the settlement projects, and creates an apartheid system with limited Palestinian sovereignty over Gaza (Erekat 2016).

The peace process has produced asymmetry between the two parties. On one hand, an asymmetry of status was created when the PLO traded recognition of Israeli territory in 78 percent of Palestine in exchange for Israeli recognition of the PLO, without defining the territory under PLO control. Israel also recognized "the political legitimate rights of the Palestinians," as included in the preamble of the Oslo Declaration of Principles (DOP) in 1993, without recognizing the Palestinian people and their right to territory. The outcome was clear: Israel's territorial boundaries were recognized, whereas the political rights of Palestinian citizens were accepted, but it territorial boundaries remained unresolved. As a result, Palestinians were disconnected from their land, leaving them without a territory, and making recognition only symbolic (Gazit, Shehadeh & Abdel Shafi 1994).

The second element of asymmetry stems from the first. After the 1967 occupied territories fell under dispute, the Israeli government used its powers to gradually reduce the Palestinian portion of the territory. By 2015, they de facto annexed two-thirds of Area C in the West Bank. In addition, the de jure annexation of East Jerusalem doubled twelve times since 1967 (Halabi 2001: 10). Beyond the annexation of land, Jewish settlers created communities in East Jerusalem and the West Bank which are now inhabited by more than 600,000 persons. 406,302 of these settlers are located in the West Bank and 200,000 in East Jerusalem, as of the end of 2014 (*Middle East Monitor* 2016).

The peace process after the 1991 Madrid Conference failed to address the issue of settlement expansion, thus creating two contradictory developments. The process focused on building trust and understanding between the negotiators on both sides with the hope that it would lead to an agreement, while settlements were simultaneously expanding. In light of tensions on the ground, and the several wars that followed this period, many speculated as to whether peace was an end goal of the process or simply a ruse. Beyond the good intentions of the international community, a negotiation process, which played out like a public relations campaign, offered Israel a needed 'time out.' During this period, the Israelis were able to create conditions in the West Bank and East Jerusalem that made a two-state solution seem like an impossibility.

The plight of the Palestinian-Israeli peace process continues to hinge on the dichotomy between credible negotiations and a parallel continuation and escalation of conflict via Israeli settlement expansion and other punitive measures conducted against Palestinians. These measures have included closures, checkpoints, detentions, and provocations at Al-Aqsa Mosque that have occurred concurrently with negotiations. Such activities have undermined the initial achievements of negotiations, but also created a situation in which negotiators were disconnected from the reality on the ground. Negotiators and third parties assumed that, regardless of the odds, they would be capable of brokering a deal and that such a deal would impact the situation on the ground. The results of negotiations have proved otherwise. Given the asymmetric relationship, Israeli negotiators lacked a sense of urgency to change the occupation into a compromise effort with their Palestinian counterparts. Instead, Israeli government practices deepened the divide to the detriment of prospects for peaceful resolution through negotiations. The United States could inspire urgency in the Israeli camp by withholding support to Israel in UN agencies or threatening to stop the flow of aid. President George H. W. Bush and his Secretary of State, James Baker, did so in the early 1990s, which brought Yitzhak Shamir to the Madrid conference in 1991.

The current situation reflects the need for a third party that is capable of creating a compliance-based process in which both parties reach for or fulfill previous agreements. Israeli compliance would include, among other commitments, a settlement freeze and a natural progression toward the 2003 Road Map to Peace. With a freeze on settlement construction, both sides would be able to negotiate from a more symmetrical position. A freeze would create trust among the Palestinians and signal that Israel does not intend on using negotiations as a false pretext for annexation of Palestinian territory. Such a process will take place "only when Israeli officialdom will be prepared to refer to the State of Israel and the State of Palestine in equal terms" (Sheleff 2005: 28).

Brief Review of the Israeli Palestinian Negotiations: The Role of the Third Party

Throughout 25 years of negotiation, two moments stand out as milestones in the path towards a final permanent status agreement: the Taba and Stockholm negotiations in 2001 (Qurie'a 2006a; Qurie'a 2006b), and the Abu Mazen (Mahmoud Abbas) and Ehud Olmert negotiations in 2008, which led to a draft agreement in July 2008. Details of the 2008 agreement may be found in Erekat (2010a), who succeeded Qurie'a (also known as Abu Ala) as the Chief Palestinian Negotiator. The government of Ariel Sharon ended the 2001 talks in 2002, while the 2008 negotiations lapsed after Olmert's decision to wage war against the Gaza Strip at the end of that year. The incursion into Gaza resulted in cancellation of the planned Israeli-Palestinian meeting with then President George W. Bush at the White House, which was scheduled for January 3, 2009 (Erekat 2010a: 6).

These two negotiations represented direct Israeli-Palestinian engagements in the absence of a third-party mediator. Interestingly, Washington-led negotiations between the Palestinian and Israeli delegations in 1992–1993 failed, yet direct secret bilateral negotiations in Oslo succeeded, as evidenced by the signing of the DOP in 1995. Palestinian President Mahmoud Abbas led the Oslo negotiations for the Palestinians. He wrote:

> The Israelis feared the Americans would kill this achievement [Oslo], as they killed the London agreement (King Hussein-Shimon Peres), due to internal American calculations, especially because the negotiations were taking place directly with the PLO.
>
> ABBAS 1994: 245

The way that these negotiations concluded suggests that Israel was not in a position to reach a peace deal with the Palestinian people. As previously mentioned, the Sharon government ended the 2001 negotiations in Taba, preventing any breakthrough, while Olmert prevented movement towards resolution by storming Gaza in 2008. Similarly, Yitzhak Rabin failed to deliver on the promise of dismantling Jewish homes built in the heart of Hebron in February 1994. This failure occurred despite widespread public opinion in favor of Israel removing the settlements. Moreover, instead of withdrawing from the West Bank in 1996 – with the exception of military bases and settlement building areas – settlement expansion continued under the Netanyahu government in violation of the interim agreement of 1995 (Oslo II). Through the Wye River memorandum in 1998, Netanyahu made a new agreement with Yasser Arafat that decreased Israeli withdrawals compared to the levels promised under Oslo II. These withdrawals, however, were never implemented. Other examples of unimplemented interim agreements made by Israeli negotiators persist. Tragically, third party mediators have refrained from taking action against such violations, despite their role as guarantor.

This opens several paths of inquiry. Why would Israel move forward if the benefits of continued occupation were better than the benefits of bringing it to an end? Why would the government of Israel confront right-wing settlers over a freeze or the dismantling of settlements? Third parties avoided taking action against these violations. Therefore, what is the motivation to take any real steps toward peace in the absence of international pressure? Also, in the absence of any real pressure on Israel to implement its obligations according to previous agreements, how can any future agreements be reached?

These issues, in addition to the concept of building negotiations around the division of 1967 occupied territories, highlight the perceptions of the two negotiating parties and their reaction to the American role in negotiations. It seems both sides mistrusted the American team each for their own reason. The Israeli team insisted on bilateral negotiations in the absence of third-party influence. This approach is based on the notion that bilateral negotiations are better for Israel in that they place more pressure on Palestinians. It is also based on the belief that developing personal relations with the Palestinian negotiators would achieve better deals for Israel. Creating trust and understanding with the Palestinian negotiators are tools that would facilitate the provisional agreements achieved between the two sides to date. In this regard, President Abbas was receptive to the trust-building approach and indicated a willingness toward "intimate relations between the negotiators of the two sides" (Abbas 1994: 15–16). Abu Ala confirmed this approach in his writings about his role as negotiator with the Palestinian delegation during the Palestinian-Israeli negotiations from Oslo 1993 to Annapolis 2007.

With regard to the Palestinian side, measures adopted up to the Camp David negotiations in 2000 sought a position that combined caution of the American position – predicated on a presumption of their bias toward Israel – and a desire to avoid American involvement. Abu Ala wrote:

> What we can get from the Israelis on the table is bigger and more important than what we can get from the Americans who appeared to us as agents of their allies [the Israelis]. In conclusion, direct negotiations with the Israeli side is more useful and precious than any negotiations that take place under the supervision of a third party, including the United States itself.
>
> QURIE'A 2006a: 8

The logic here is clear: if Americans are agents of the Israelis, then they lack the objectivity to mediate the conflict. Therefore, why are they included in talks? Instead, the belief was that negotiations should occur exclusively with the Israelis.

At a later stage, Palestinians became more amenable to American involvement in the negotiations, mainly after the Annapolis Conference. After 2007, the Palestinians began demanding American involvement, while at the same time seeking greater parity with the Israelis. In this regard, Abu Ala critiqued the stance of Secretary of State, Condoleezza Rice, who presented American proposals and then retracted them after hearing that Olmert did not support the immediate and parallel implementation of obligations by both sides, dictated by the first stage of the Roadmap for Peace (Abu Ala 2014: 51). Abu Ala also criticized the American administration for its inability to fulfill a promise made at the Annapolis Conference to present a document to the UN Security Council (UNSC) in an effort to reach a resolution (Abu Ala 2014: 162).

Erekat wrote extensively about Israeli-Palestinian negotiations and the rounds that took place during the two terms of President Barack Obama. Similarly, much of his criticism was directed at American bias towards Israel. He highlights the American practice of coordinating with Israel when drafting positions that were subsequently communicated as uniquely American. He also criticized the agreement between Senator Mitchell and Netanyahu to resume negotiations from scratch instead of starting from the point that Olmert and Abu Mazen had reached, while adding pressure on Palestine to refrain from applying for UN membership. The protest that ensued from Palestine's 2011 acceptance to join UNESCO resulted in the US cutting off aid to the UN agency once Palestine had been accepted as a member.

Many non-Palestinians also voiced their assessment of US bias toward Israel, including an account of the 2000 Camp David negotiations (Agha & Malley 2001). The authors recount the failure of President Clinton to hold Ehud Barak to a previously agreed upon phased withdrawal by Israel in accordance with prior agreements regarding settlement removal from Palestinian occupied territory. During the conference, President Clinton coordinated first with Barak, before presenting to Arafat, whom he promised not to blame for the failure to reach peace. Clinton, however, did ultimately blame Arafat.

Haaretz journalist Barak Ravid also addressed concerns of bias in an investigation into the 2013–2014 Kerry Initiative. Ravid reviewed the Initiative, showing that the position of Mahmoud Abbas was neglected. The American team worked with the Israeli team to develop a framework agreement without conferring with the Palestinians. The result was a 10-page document that addressed issues of permanent status. While copies of the initiative existed at the State Department in Washington, DC, and a few other offices in Jerusalem, the document was never presented to the Palestinians (Ravid 2014: 16). President Abbas was shocked by the brazen nature of the document when it was presented to him verbally by Secretary Kerry in a February 2014 meeting in Paris (Ravid 2014: 17).

Constructionist Approach to Transform the Conflict toward the Two-State Solution

Lessons from the past can serve as a starting point for future American intervention in the Israeli-Palestinian conflict. The main lesson learned is that realism does not work and that a transformative constructionist approach is required. The realism approach has been used in the Palestinian-Israeli conflict for the last 25 years. The starting point for realism is power and interest. Israel, as a state, enjoys an upper hand over the stateless Palestinians. Of note is the fact that realism was not the approach of Track 2 Israeli-Palestinian engagements beginning in the 1960s (Kaufman, Walidet & Verhoeven 2006). But it has been the American approach to mediation since Madrid in 1991, giving Israeli demands more credibility. Israeli-created settlements in the West Bank have become bargaining chips. Discussions focus on which parts of the territory should be kept and which should be annexed by Israel, instead of focusing on providing settlers the option to stay in a Palestinian state as citizens of Palestine or to migrate back to Israel.

Realism also favors Israel at the expense of the Palestinians by designating Jerusalem as the capital of Israel, while granting Palestinians control over certain areas of the city, such as Al-Haram Al-Sharif. Another issue relates to territorial swaps. These have occurred as a result of the establishment of Israeli settlements and have been supported by what Israel deems its security needs. But such security concerns are reserved for only one party.

Palestinians have also been asked to be realistic about the right of return for refugees to Israel, and to accept that only a symbolic number of refugees may ever be given the right to go back to Israel. These rights, of course, will remain subject to Israeli approval and involve a complex formula consisting of eligibility, criteria and numbers. Palestinians were asked to recognize Israel as a Jewish State, which automatically eliminated the rights of Palestinian refugees and, at the same time, put at risks the rights of Palestinian citizens of Israel.

This realism has had three main problems since the beginning of negotiations between the two sides. The first is that it dealt with the West Bank, East Jerusalem and Gaza Strip as areas under dispute, not areas where a Palestinian state could live in peace and security beside Israel. Second, it accepted the asymmetry in power relations between the two sides, recognizing Israeli facts created in East Jerusalem and the West Bank as irreversible, and therefore a bargaining chip between the two sides. Finally, the Palestinian state's size, territory, borders, date of establishment, and political, economic and security structures, are all topics subject to Israeli approval through specified negotiation parameters. This has given Israel veto power over the establishment of the Palestinian state based on 1967 borders over the last 24 years of negotiation. In this regard, Israel accepted the establishment of a Palestinian state, but not in accordance with 1967 borders, with East Jerusalem as its capital, or with sovereignty over borders. The annexation of large blocks of land for Israeli settlements continued, while a solution to the Palestinian refugee problem is continually ignored. With these reservations, the Israeli proposal is less about creating a Palestinian state alongside Israel and more about creating a Palestinian state based on land leftover after Israeli annexation of East Jerusalem and the settlement blocks.

This realism is contradictory not only to the UN Charter and UN resolutions pertaining to the Palestinian-Israeli conflict, but also to the spirit of the Oslo agreement. As it stands (circa 2015), the establishment of a Palestinian state within this framework has led to the creation of a larger Israel or what Erekat (2015: 16) calls, "one state, two systems." Israeli control spreads across most of historic Palestine, with two different systems in place: one for Israelis, including settlers living in on Palestinian territory, and another for Palestinians, who are discriminated against on their own lands. The outcome of this realism is a win-lose position that considers a two-state solution increasingly at risk as Israel expands into Palestinian territories. Are such facts reversible? Within the framework of realism, they lead to deepening divides and the growth of Israel at the expense of a collective transfer of Palestinians.

The solution proposed here is a constructionist transformative approach for American engagement to solve the Palestinian-Israeli conflict. This approach is constructionist because it aims at creating a historical process for the construction of the state of Palestine by the United States.[1]

As constructionism might fall into the trap of relativism, it is combined here with the transformative approach. This approach aims to bring about structural changes within institutions which would do away with violence and asymmetry. In this sense, the transformative approach is one that includes bottom-up processes that build the political, economic and social structures of the weaker side in the conflict. In addition, it also fosters rights-based relationships between the antagonist parties (Galtung 2014; Lederach 2003; Ramsbotham, Woodhouse & Miall 2008: 29).

Such a constructionist transformative approach differs from realism, which focuses on the use of power – mainly physical – to solve conflicts through top-down processes. A constructionist transformative approach would require the United States to use its power and leverage, but at the same time requires that it not limit its role to the use of that leverage.

In the Israeli-Palestinian conflict, such an approach would have several characteristics. The first is that it would transform the conflict from a protracted or intractable conflict (Ramsbotham, Woodhouse & Miall 2008: 43–47, 84–89)

---

1 Constructionism is different from constructivism as a result of its focus on history and the role of social rather than individual actors (Delanty 2005: 140; Andrews 2012).

because it does not recognize the facts created on the ground as being irreversible. For example, such facts could include those that separated East and West Germany with the Berlin Wall or those that created the French settlement projects in Algeria, both of which were ultimately reversed. Israel also reversed the settlement project in Gaza with a decision by Prime Minister Sharon in 2005. The same is true of the Israeli separation barrier in the West Bank, which could be dismantled or rebuilt at 1967 borders, instead of inside the territory of the West Bank. Moreover, the Israeli settlement projects could also be brought to an end fully or partly if there is political will.

The second characteristic is that such an approach would allow the United States to create a multilevel system of top-down and bottom-up approaches (i.e., economic, political, security) working with international, regional and local actors through bilateral and trilateral levels of implementation. The multi-track approach (Diamond & McDonald 1996) would consist of different partnerships (for example, one for officials and parliamentarians, one composed of officials and civil society, one of former officials, one composed solely of civil society actors, and a final track composed of spoilers or rejectionists of the peace process). Lederach suggests these interventions need to be made by top leaders, intermediate leaders and grassroots leaders through a complex methodology involving dialogue, mediation, arbitration, coercion, pressure, and peacemaking and peacebuilding interventions (Ramsbotham, Woodhouse & Miall 2008: 24).

The leading assumption of the transformative constructionist approach is that positive peace (Galtung 2014: 52–63) is based on the creation of a structure of political, economic and cultural interactions between former antagonists, and a fair distribution of justice. This structure facilitates the transformation of the conflict. A second assumption is that through the creation of the appropriate construct for action (Habermas 1981), the accumulation of short-term, medium-term and long-term interventions will lead to the achievement of planned objectives. Therefore, this study argues that the ideal approach to solving the Israeli-Palestinian conflict is a shift away from the American realist approach to one based on mutual justice and fairness.

US Construct of the State of Palestine

The transformative constructionist approach must begin with a paradigm shift and change in methodology. The paradigm shift should be in two directions. The first consists of freeing the establishment of the State of Palestine from

Israeli will, internal calculations, competitions, and internal political bargaining. This feat could be accomplished by adopting an American plan for the creation of the Palestinian state. This plan could be based on Wilsonian principles and the American King Crane Committee established in 1919, which recommended maintaining Greater Syrian unity and ebbing the flow of Jewish immigration (Fawcett 2013). This plan can be adapted by the United States to fit current facts on the ground. At the same time, the plan can call for a settlement freeze in the occupied territories of 1967 centered on the notion of freedom.

The second paradigm shift, which is more important, would require a shift in US views of the conflict as a division of 1967 occupied territories between the two sides to an approach that considers the 1967 occupied territories to be Palestinian. Once recognized, the discourse can focus on finding equitable solutions to legitimate issues. These issues include an arrangement to allow Jews the freedom to worship at the Wailing Wall in Jerusalem, the return of the Jewish Quarter in the Old City of Jerusalem to its 1948 size of 5 *donums* (without the additional parts added after 1967), the unification of villages divided in 1948 between Israel and West Bank such as Barta'a close to Jenin city and Beit Safafa of Jerusalem, in addition to swapped areas for refugee return (Shaath 2006: 21), and the creation of a corridor allowing free movement for Palestinian people between West Bank and Gaza Strip through Israel. Land swaps for settlements created in the West Bank cannot be added to this list. These settlements are illegitimate according to international law, as is keeping Israeli forces in the Palestinian territory under the guise of security needs. This is a position that will not be accepted by Palestinian leadership, which alternatively accepted the deployment of international forces along the borders of Palestine with both Jordan and Israel.

These paradigm shifts require American-Palestinian engagement to clarify uncertain terms and implement common understanding. This may be achievable by creating a sustainable American-Palestinian strategic dialogue, similar to the decades-long Israeli-American relationship. This dialogue must replace the US dictating to Palestinians what is best for them to solve permanent status issues with Israel. These issues include suggestions of dividing the 1967 occupied territories between the two sides, as occurred at Camp David in 2000 and through the Kerry initiative. The US could take a new approach, considering the 1967 borders to be the basis for any negotiations. In addition, they could work towards a solution to the Palestinian refugee problem. Opening avenues for strategic dialogue with Palestinian leaders would allow for an articulation of requests for future parameters – rather than relying on previously suggested American parameters that were closer to Israeli positions.

Time is quickly disappearing for any real approach that would change the events on the ground between Palestinians and Israelis. The two-state solution is on the edge of being lost to realism through Israeli settlement expansion and the annexation policy. It has been 100 years since Britain's Balfour Declaration in 1917 and the Sykes Picot agreement that split the territory in 1916. In addition to a shift in approach, a new methodology is required. US adoption of the establishment of a Palestinian state on 1967 borders, with border modifications to be made only for legitimate humanitarian reasons, needs to be combined with a methodology of continuing engagement with the Palestinians, the Israelis, the Arabs, and the international community. This engagement could include a combined political, economic and security track. The following is a brief description of how each of these tracks can work, followed by a description of how they can work together.

The Political Process Reconstructed

The history of both the conflict and previous agreements teaches us that any political process leading to the creation of the State of Palestine has to include three components. The first of these are two short-term components that both encourage the implementation of previous agreements and the rebuilding of Gaza Strip infrastructure following the three devastating wars of 2008, 2011 and 2014. The longer-term component has to do with the political process to put the State of Palestine on the world map beside Israel.

The fulfillment of these obligations from previous agreements is not something that needs to wait until both sides reach a final status agreement, as has been advised by the Israeli government. Instead, it is up to the US to create a mechanism for encouraging both sides to fulfill their obligations, which are not limited to stopping violence and building state institutions on the Palestinian side. On the Israeli side, freezing settlement expansion, dismantling settlement outposts, withdrawing from all of the West Bank (excluding military camps), creating free passage between the West Bank and Gaza, and reopening Palestinian institutions in East Jerusalem closed by Israel are important steps to be achieved. As a guarantor to previous agreements, the US is in a position to ensure these obligations are implemented without further delay.

With regard to rebuilding Gaza, the US might sponsor indirect negotiations working toward uniting a Palestinian delegation that consists of all the Palestinian factions, including Hamas. With Israel, this united delegation could discuss all Gaza issues, within a certain timeframe, to reach an agreement. Indirect negotiations between a united Palestinian delegation and Israel already took place in Cairo in 2014, but ended due to problematic relations between Egypt and Hamas. The US could decide to use this opportunity of having a united Palestinian delegation to negotiate with Israel about Gazan issues, sponsoring negotiations or engaging Egypt to spur the resumption of talks. The US could either chair these negotiations or encourage Egypt to get involved, but it is crucial that an unbiased third-party intervener recognize Hamas, and acknowledge that it is part of the social fabric of Palestinian society and not merely a terrorist organization (Roy 2011).

In 1994, Hamas accepted the establishment of a Palestinian state on 1967 borders (Al-Shaer 1999). Despite the fact that Hamas is not ready to recognize Israel, it is ready to agree to a long-term *hudna* (*Der Spiegel* 2006), defined in Islam as an agreed-upon cessation of hostilities for a set period of time. Hamas leaders have already expressed readiness to stick to nonviolence as a method of protesting the end of occupation (Solomon 2009). The concept of *hudna* includes a readiness to sit at a negotiation table to discuss terms where Israel is free to present a plan for a peaceful resolution. Hamas has engaged in official indirect negotiations with Israel since 2008. In Gaza, Hamas has proven its ability to bring factions into compliance, with a ceasefire occurring with Israel under a prior *hudna* agreement. Hamas has also been fighting terrorist groups such as ISIL in the Yarmouk refugee camp in Syria and Salafi Jihadi groups in Gaza. These efforts included an attack on a mosque in Rafah in 2009 led by Abdul al-Latif Mousa after he declared an Islamic emirate. For these reasons, engagement with Hamas over Gaza is necessary to clamp down on Salafi Jihadi groups waging violent extremist attacks in the area, and open relations regionally to groups such as the Muslim Brotherhood in Syria and Yemen.

The US should engage Hamas, in particular, on issues related to the Gaza Strip, but also in unifying the Palestinian delegation. Permanent status issues with Israel have fallen solely on PLO leadership, which Hamas has accepted in the past through various statements, suggesting they are not interested in negotiating an end to conflict with Israel. The 2006 Mecca Agreement with Fatah and Hamas left permanent status negotiations to the PLO and outlined a plan to hold a referendum on any final agreement with Israel (Abu-Khalaf et al. 2009). Ultimately, Hamas and Fatah agreed to abide by the results of the referendum, even if these results contradicted their political positions. In this regard, it is a double standard for Americans to accept Israeli rightwing extremist groups such as Habayit Hayehudi, led by Naftali Bennett on the one hand, and on the other to refuse to recognize prior agreements and governing committees such as the PLO, and rebuff Hamas due to its failure to recognize the State of Israel. A nonpartisan American approach might call for both Hamas and

Habayit Hayehudi to commit to nonviolence while both remain free to continue their ideological positions of non-recognition of the other side until a permanent status agreement may be achieved. This will require an easing of the Middle East Quartet for Peace's (including the United Nations, the United States, the European Union and Russia) three conditions on Hamas[2] and non-use of the US veto against Palestinian unity.

Putting Palestine on the Map

Another political component puts Palestine on the map as an internationally recognized entity with clear border demarcations that adhere to the 1967 borders. This move is not at odds with the resumption of negotiations with Israel, as it aims to create the symmetry required for successful negotiations. With regard to international recognition, it has been proposed that the US will conclude, after years of negotiations, that granting Palestine full UN membership is a necessary means to push the Israeli government beyond the current status quo. This change will foster fruitful and productive negotiations that take into consideration the needs and interests of both sides. The US could propose a UNSC resolution that includes elevating Palestine to UN membership. Also, the US could support a UN General Assembly initiative to establish a second special UN Commission for Palestine (UNSCOP-2). This commission would be similar to UNSCOP of 1947 (Segal 2012), but would not deal with the fate of historical Palestine. Instead, it would investigate the reasons behind the delay of achieving the Palestinian people's right of self-determination, the right of return for Palestinian refugees, and bring forward proposals that address facts on the ground in Palestine.

Additionally, the US could support Palestinian membership in UN organizations, and allow Palestinians to bring legal suits to the International Criminal Court related to Israeli settlement expansion in the Palestinian occupied territories of West Bank and East Jerusalem. These measures would help keep the two-state solution alive. Other components of a US draft resolution to the UNSC could also include a call for a trilateral process that ensures inclusive fulfillment of obligations according to previous agreements within a specified

2 The three conditions outlined by the Quartet are as follows: A Palestinian state must recognize the state of Israel without prejudging what various grievances or claims are appropriate, abide by previous diplomatic agreements, and renounce violence as a means of achieving goals.

timeframe, – in addition to the reconstruction of Gaza, the resumption of negotiations over the two-state solution, and a solution to the refugee problem. The non-fulfillment of Israeli peace agreement obligations contributes to the exacerbation of the asymmetry between the two sides. This would not be a renegotiation. Earlier resolutions from negotiations would be on the table that illustrate border advancements and ways of developing modalities for implementing the previously agreed upon understandings, such as the contentious issue of Palestinian refugees.

A UNSC resolution would also lead to comprehensive peace in the Middle East based on the Arab Peace Initiative (API), combined with the creation of a Middle East free from weapons of mass destruction. The League of Arab States would ideally create the basis for the API. It could foster support for the Israeli-Palestinian negotiations that includes the concerned Arab countries of Egypt, Jordan, Saudi Arabia, and Morocco by creating a support committee modeled on the Middle East Quartet. This Arab committee would have a monitoring role in the negotiations and would intervene in cooperation with the Middle East Quartet, when necessary.

A Security Council resolution would create a new climate by promoting a paradigm shift toward a new type of negotiation aimed at discussing the implementation of previously agreed upon solutions rather than renegotiating. Once the resolution is adopted, attention can center on an international conference to launch the peace process through the formation of a follow up committee working in tandem with the Quartet as an auxiliary component managing negotiations. Along with the previously mentioned Arab countries, the BRICS and Japanese could ensure international responsibility towards the peace process through a cooperative process that moves beyond the US taking on the primary responsibility for enforcement and implementation. Ideally, a process of collective facilitation would maintain shared responsibility.

During the allotted time frame of negotiations, parties would work on fulfilling their obligations from previous agreements. The Quartet would support a working group through which both sides identify their obligations, create a timeframe, and work toward full implementation. The international community could make use of financial incentives (grants or loans) in the form of carrots or sticks (sanctions) to encourage parties to move toward full implementation of a peacebuilding plan.

Once negotiations are finalized and an agreement is reached, withdrawal of Israeli occupying forces would need to take place within three years. International peacekeeping and peacebuilding forces will deploy in the areas where Israel withdraws for an interim period to help preserve security (that is, peacekeeping), and build stable institutions to ensure a prosperous Palestinian independence (that is, peacebuilding), in a way similar to the case in East Timor. If the Israeli government fails to move forward on any of these political tracks, then the US should use tools to pressure Israel, such as abstaining from using their veto during Security Council resolutions that condemn Israel's actions in occupied Palestinian territories, freezing financial support, or halting military and security cooperation. Moreover, civil society can be engaged in a participatory peacemaking and peacebuilding process through Track 1.5, Track 2, and Track 3 efforts.

The Economic Track for Constructing the Palestinian State

This track is about creating Palestinian facts on the ground and is currently hindered by a lack of full control over territory and self-determination. Prior experience suggests that economic prosperity in the State of Palestine is impossible in the face of restrictions imposed on development by Israel within Area C (currently consisting of two thirds of the West Bank) and East Jerusalem. Furthermore, free passage between the West Bank and Gaza Strip, along with free trade between Palestine and the Arab and Islamic world via Egypt and Jordan, are necessary for long-term economic growth in Palestine.

The continuation of harsh Israeli restrictions places any attempt to build a prosperous State of Palestine with a viable economy in jeopardy. In the West Bank and East Jerusalem, ongoing contradictory processes adopted post-1967 prioritize the economic development of the Jewish sector to the detriment of the Palestinian territories. These territories have been subjected to ethnic cleansing and the expropriation of space, territory and landscape. Evacuation of the Palestinian Bedouins from Area C (BIMKOM 2009), and the confiscation of identity cards from East Jerusalem Palestinians are two examples of the ethnic cleansing policies Israel has employed. Palestinians have been made impotent through limits on economic development, and fallen prey to a process of systematic destruction by an opposing power. This process has led to the de-development of a local indigenous economy through the combination of forced acts of transfer and ethnic cleansing.

Previous economic practices of the international community focused on building the State of Palestine from the bottom up through focused efforts on strengthening the capacities of the Palestinian Authority (PA) to ensure continuation of PA employee salaries, supporting the Palestinian security sector, and supporting Palestinian development projects in Area C (subject to Israeli permit approval) and East Jerusalem. The Gaza Strip was left without a real development strategy due to fears that development funds might support Hamas.

The US$5.7 billion in aid allocated for Gaza reconstruction at the Sharm el-Sheikh conference in March 2009 was put on hold for that reason, and the same was true for aid pledged to the rebuilding of Gaza after the 2014 war with Israel.

At the Annapolis conference of 2007, US President George W. Bush promised the creation of a Palestinian State by 2009. Dr. Salam Fayyad (2009), former Prime Minister of Palestine, implemented a policy of development of the Palestinian state and its institutions through a bottom-up process that ignores Israeli restrictions imposed on the Palestinian territories in Area C and East Jerusalem. During the seven-year period of Fayyad government rule, emphasis was placed on projects in those areas. Furthermore, the government released quarterly reports about the number of projects implemented. By 2011, the World Bank presented a report on Fayyad's achievements, and concluded that these efforts were a clear sign that Palestinians were ready for statehood.

Potential reasons for the lack of progress toward statehood include the fact that the Fayyad Government was unable to facilitate any major development in Gaza due to the unwillingness of the international community to offer aid to Hamas. Secondly, Fayyad's attempts at creating sovereign projects in Area C, such as an airport in the Jordan Valley, were never realized because Israel stood in the way of Palestinian development. When Fayyad built without Israeli approval, Israel would demolish it. This in part explains why he was unable to put in place significant projects in East Jerusalem. The international community failed to either provide appropriate support to Fayyad or apply the pressure needed on Israel to clear the way for Palestinian development projects in Area C and East Jerusalem. Ultimately, Fayyad's attempts on the ground were overshadowed by a lack of political success in reaching an agreement that supported commonality between Israeli and Palestinian interests.

The root causes for such failure are again related to that which has stalled all previous attempts at the peace process: occupation of the Palestinian territories after 1967. Asymmetry between Israelis and Palestinians limits growth. As Israeli expansion into Palestinian territories continues, Palestinian building development is limited through the use of a strict permit system reserved solely for Palestinians. The practice of demolishing Palestinian infrastructure built without a permit is at the heart of this inequality. For many, it is reasonable to assume that Israelis and Palestinians living side-by-side both share the right to build on their own land. Unfortunately, this is not the case. The international community, along with the Office of the Quartet in Jerusalem, have adapted to and worked within Israeli restrictions in an effort to support Palestinian development. Sadly, development in Gaza has ground to a halt due to Israel's unwillingness to work with Hamas. Beyond these failures, the Kerry Initiative of 2014 included US$4 billion in developmental aid for Palestine through public and private sector cooperation. The plan focused on several promising projects in Area C, such as developing a potassium company at the Dead Sea and further developing tourism projects. The plan failed due to a breakdown in negotiations, which sent a message of political uncertainty to the private sector, and a corresponding reluctance of businesses to develop in a time of turmoil.

Based on these experiences, a new approach for economic development in Palestine can be promoted by US as a mediator to move beyond Israeli restrictions imposed in Area C and East Jerusalem. This approach can include macroeconomic development projects included in the Kerry Initiative, but also micro projects focused on participatory community development, an approach that is central to Palestinian tradition. These projects have the benefit of being sustainable and self-reliant. It has been suggested that the US can take charge of these community initiatives by coordinating with NGOs and humanitarian aid agencies working on the ground, in addition to following up with the Israeli government in an effort to prevent inappropriate limits.

The Security Track for Constructing the State of Palestine

The security track is another field that requires a shift in approach and perspective. During the period of the peace process, the security of the State of Palestine was a non-issue. The central concern has been the security of Israel. Within that frame work, the independent security of Palestine is considered only to the extent to which it relates to Israeli interests. Therefore, a tradeoff occurs between the independence of Palestine and the security of Israel. Along these lines, the State of Palestine is not allowed to create an army, but instead a lightly armed security force, with Israel maintaining control over state and eastern borders. Additionally, Israel controls all advanced emergency and security warning stations, adopts the right to enter Palestinian territory at will, and controls the air and naval space in and around Palestinian territory. This grants Israel the freedom to fly through Palestinian skies whenever it chooses.

Limiting security concerns to the preferences of Israelis along with tethering the independence of Palestine to the fulfillment of Israeli security preferences does not signal openness to a permanent status agreement. In this regard, Palestinians have displayed a high level of flexibility by accepting the deployment of international forces on the borders of the State of Palestine. Of course, the issue of Palestinian sovereignty over its security affairs pervades discourse on the conflict. One state should not exclude the rights of another based on their own security concerns, especially since Palestine faces similar security threats from terrorist groups. Palestine lacks the wherewithal to confront this terrorism, as it has no army, proper training or equipment for its security forces. It must rely on cooperation from international forces deployed in Palestine to confront sanctioned acts of terror. The idea of Palestine depending on Israel for its security concerns is not well received on the Palestinian side because it further entrenches Israeli occupation.

Therefore, there are loud calls for the US to help develop a new approach to security in Palestine and Israel based on the principle that security is important and that no party should be excluded from planning and development protocols. This approach requires that Israeli security concerns should not hamper, freeze or supersede Palestine's right to ensure its own security and prosperity. Consequently, both sides should engage in a process to find equitable solutions for their respective security concerns. Security vulnerabilities need not be limited to security of the state, land, sea and borders, but should also include human security. Addressing collective security of Palestinian and Israeli women and children against fear, killing, disposition, transfer and injury is no less important than the protection of borders and good governance. Furthermore, security requires professional training. The idea that Israeli security forces are the only forces competent enough to undertake security protocols is myopic. Additionally, refusing to work with Palestinian partners on coordinated efforts limits avenues of cooperation between the two peoples and, more broadly, with members of the international community. In this regard, the PA has a well-established track record of capably protecting Israel from attacks since 2007. In recent years, Hamas has also joined in preventing attacks against Israel from Gaza. Why then does Israel not respect the capabilities of Palestinians to act accordingly in their own security interests?

The issue that continues to surface in response to this question relates to the possibility of regional attacks that require Israel to maintain strict eastern borders control. Shaul Arieli, a security expert, responded to this idea, saying that Israel can develop an anti-missile defense system without keeping the Jordan Valley under its control.[3] Moreover, Israel can establish effective security cooperation with Palestinian security and international forces, which will strengthen Israel's ability to face security threats without employing an occupying force in the Jordan Valley. The United States could support discussions along these lines, shifting to an approach to security that transcends Israeli-Palestinian divides to include the issue of Palestinian security. A US plan could, first, present Palestinian security, as Sayigh (1995) suggests, as a matrix that promotes security by developing Palestinian well-being through development

3 See online at www.shaularieli.com.

projects, democracy and human rights promotion, and an effective security force that meets the needs of Palestinian security concerns. Creating a US-led peacekeeping/peacebuilding force can help Palestine preserve security and build supportive democratic institutions (Salem 2007: 180). This force could also be comprised of experts in development from Arab countries.

Finally, one cannot leave the security track without viewing the regional security component. Regional threats have led Israel to accept the deployment of massive Egyptian security forces in the Sinai to confront terrorist groups operating in the area. This example might offer the basis for Palestine to argue that protecting its needs requires similar actions. On the other hand, considerable animus has surfaced in the Middle East surrounding the P5+1 agreement with Iran. Iran raises the issue of instability in the region, particularly regarding the notion of promoting a Middle East region that is free from weapons of mass destruction. Egypt continues to highlight this issue with the aim of diffusing the threat of Israeli nuclear weapons. Greater symmetry in the region might push Israel toward considering the beneficial prospects of a sustainable peace agreement with the Palestinian people and other countries in the region.

Conclusion: Three Tracks Together

Arouri has claimed that "the role of the sole peacemaker has started to reach its end" (2012, p. 124), but it has not. This article has focused on a potential future where the US assumes a "going for broke" stance on the Israeli-Palestinian conflict by accepting the creation of a Palestinian state and a new third-party approach to get there. Camp David in 2000, the Olmert-Abu Mazen negotiations, and the Annapolis Conference of 2007 were all unsuccessful due to failures to conceive of a Palestinian state with sovereignty over East Jerusalem, an absence of an agreed solution to the Palestinian refugee problem, Israeli control of eastern borders, the continuation of settlement building and Israeli annexations. Offering these approaches once again will not help since many past issues remain unresolved. One might argue that Israel was established without final boarders and that Palestine might follow the same path. Such an argument contradicts the fact that what is needed in the framework of a permanent status agreement is demarcation of a final and agreed upon border between the two-states of Palestine and Israel.

Construction of dual transformative processes that facilitate top-down and bottom-up change in an effort to create the State of Palestine is required. Pressures concentrated from below will support Palestinian development in all occupied territories of 1967 without excluding Areas A and B of the West Bank. Additionally, supporting nonviolent Palestinian resistance to occupation, rebuilding the Gaza Strip, and requiring Israel to fulfill its obligations from previous negotiations will facilitate Palestinian development in the areas Israel currently occupies. It will also open up resources from Arab countries as well as international funding to further the development process.

The main issues in the Israeli-Palestinian conflict are territorial, not simply trust or mistrust between parties. In the case of Palestinian and Israeli negotiators, trust was present between the negotiators. The problem was a win-lose scenario on the ground, caused by rapid settlement expansion and land grabs that Palestinians could not overcome – in part, a problem between occupier and occupied. Golan (2007: 142) has suggested that "a case can nonetheless be made for the possibility that the two sides will opt for realism – leaving the issue of trust to a later stage – and adopt something quite close to the peace plans that have emerged."

The means for reaching a peace agreement should not be focused around negotiations and bringing the parties back to the table with preconditions, as called for in Quartet statements. The solution lies in moving beyond asymmetry by recognizing Palestine in the UN and creating political, economic and security tracks to build Palestinian infrastructure through multilateral processes. By generating symmetry, the status of Palestine will emerge, allowing its leaders to negotiate borders and refugee issues with Israel on the basis of relative parity.

These three tracks need to be reinforced together. For the economic track to succeed, Israel will need to fulfill its obligations from previous agreements. This includes a phased withdrawal from 1967 occupied territories in the West Bank (except military camps and settlements), a commitment Israel made in the 1995 interim agreement that was supposed to be completed within 18 months. Furthermore, the establishment of the State of Palestine should not be held hostage to Israeli security paranoia. Galtung (2015: 80) illustrates that "The dominant paradigm in inter-nation, inter-state affairs is still 'security studies,' academically institutionalized paranoia," which aligns with the current Israeli approach to security and the practice of limiting security cooperation with Palestinian counterparts and international actors. In seeking to resolve the ongoing Israeli-Palestinian conflict, a US approach to security is needed both in concept and in practice, as limited time remains to rescue the two-state solution.

Diamond and McDonald (1996) developed the multi-track method, which the new US model could evoke, seeking to be inclusive of the economic, security and political tracks. Such inclusion would complicate the task ahead for the United States. But without the economic and security tracks that aim to create symmetry between the sides, the political process is likely to fail. The new US approach needs to be participatory and include global blocks, Middle Eastern countries, and civil society actors.

Epilogue

US President Donald Trump took office after the preparation of this article. Many journalistic and policy-based articles have been written speculating on what he might do regarding Middle East peace or offering advice to lobby the president and his team. We hope that the new president views this article as advocating for a new approach for American third-party intervention in the Israeli-Palestinian conflict, rather than an analysis of past policy. Importantly, the new administration might consider two essential elements in formulating this new mediation approach for the US. First, Trump's "art of the deal" (1987) focuses on economic deal making, not political deal making. When trying to broker a political deal, there are often many non-economic issues that must to be taken into consideration. This is certainly true in the case of the Israeli-Palestinian conflict, as we have discussed in this article.

Second, the alternatives to the two-state solution are all problematic. Transforming the West Bank from its current situation of de facto annexation to become a de jure annexation to Israel will leave the Palestinian right to self-determination unsolved, and trigger a continuation of the conflict. Moreover, Jordan will not accept annexation of parts of the West Bank to Jordan, and Egypt seeks safe and secure borders with Gaza, not annexation of its territory. Alternatives of "one country, two-states" (Kelman & Segal 2014) are all versions of the two-state solution with open borders and freedom of movement. To them, the country is perceived as a place where two peoples have attachments to the whole. Disregarding the details of these proposals, it seems possible to implement them only after crafting a territorial deal and after sustained peace and security between the two-states resulting from territorial compromise (Spears 2014).

Federal or confederal solutions in all forms, including the bi-national state formula and the one state solution, are problematic due to their recognition of existing facts on the grounds that have resulted through land grabs and settlement expansion at the expense of the Palestinians.

As a result, the two-state solution should be a priority for any future US mediation attempt. The proposed approach should combine promotion of a principles-based political process and leveraging of US influence to achieve it

Hopefully, this process will alleviate asymmetry between the parties and create better conditions for a fair solution that is based on parity.

References

Abbas, Mahmoud (2011). *The Path of Oslo*. 2nd edition. Ramallah: Bailasan Publisher.

Abu-Khalaf, I., R. Friedrich, J. Loetscher, A. Luethold, N. Masson and K. Naseef (2009). *Towards Palestinian Reconciliation*. Geneva: Center for Security Development and the Rule of Law. Available online at: http://www.dcaf.ch/towards-palestinian-national-reconciliation.

Agha, H. and R. Malley (2001). "Camp David: The Tragedy of Errors." *The New York Review of Books*. August 9. Available online at: http://www.nybooks.com/articles/2001/08/09/camp-david-the-tragedy-of-errors.

Al Shaer, Nasser Eddin (1999). *The Israeli Palestinian Peace Process: Islamic Point of View*. Nablus: Palestine Research and Studies Center.

Andrews, Tom (2012). "What Is Social Constructionism?" *Grounded Theory Review* 11, 1. Available online at: http://groundedtheoryreview.com/2012/06/01/what-is-social-constructionism.

Aruri, Naseer (2012). "Is the Two-states Solution Still Possible?" In Hani Ahmad Faris, editor, *The One State Solution to the Arab-Israeli Conflict*. Beirut: Center of Arab Unity Studies.

BIMKOM (2009). "The Prohibited Area." Available online at: http://bimkom.org/eng/the-prohibited-zone/.

Chomsky, Noam (1999). *The Fateful Triangle, United States, Israel and the Palestinians*. London: Pluto Press.

Delanty, Gerard (2005). *Social Science: Philosophical and Methodological Foundations, 2nd edition*. Maidenhead, UK: Open University Press.

Der Spiegel (2006). "Interview with Ismail Haniyeh." June 12. Accessed at: www.spiegel.de.

Diamond, Louise and John McDonald (1996). *Multi-Track Diplomacy: A Systems Approach to Peace*, 3rd edition. Boulder, CO: Kumarian Press.

Erekat, Saeb (2010a). *Special Report, Proximity Talks – and the Pressures to Move to Direct Talks* (study 3). Ramallah: PLO, the Palestinian National Authority, Negotiations Affairs Department.

Erekat, Saeb (2010b). *Special Report, the Blocked Direct Talks – and Options* (Study No. 4), Ramallah: PLO, the Palestinian National Authority, Negotiations Affairs Department.

Erekat, Saeb (2010c). *Special Report, the Political Situation in the Light of US Proposals and Decisions of the Government of Israel on Settlements and the Arab and International Positions* (study 2). Ramallah: PLO, the Palestinian National Authority, Negotiations Affairs Department.

Erekat, Saeb (2013). *The Plan, the Truth, the Crossroad, and the Fateful Decisions*, Study No. 13. Ramallah: PLO, the Palestinian National Authority, Negotiations Affairs Department.

Erekat, Saeb (2015). "Israeli-Palestinian Relations: Point of No Return." *Palestine-Israel Journal* 20, 2–3: 12–20.

Erekat, Saeb (2016). *The New Map of the Region*, study No. 18. Ramallah: PLO, the Palestinian National Authority, Negotiations Affairs Department.

Fawcett, Louise (2013). *The International Relations of the Middle East.* Oxford: Oxford University Press.

Fayyad, Salam (2009). *Two Years Path to the Palestinian Statehood.* The Palestinian National Authority.

Galtung, Johan (2015). *Clash of Civilizations? Solving Underlying Conflicts.* Kuala Lumpur: Transcend University Press.

Gazit, Shlomo, R. Shehadeh and H. Abdel Shafi (1994). "Challenges Facing Palestinian Society in the Interim Period." Jerusalem: Jerusalem Media and Communication Center. Accessed at: http://www.jmcc.org/Documentsandmaps.aspx?id=629.

Gerges, Fawaz (2013). *Obama and the Middle East: The End of the American Moment.* New York: St. Martin's Griffin.

Golan, Galia (2007). *Israel and Palestine Peace Plans from Oslo to Disengagement.* Princeton, NJ: Markus Weiner Publisher.

Grinberg, Lev (2007). *Imagined Peace: The Dynamics of Political Space in Israel Palestine.* Ramallah: Madar Center for Israeli Studies.

Halabi, Usama (2001). *The Limits of the Space and the Human Being Existence: The Geographical and the Demographic Dimensions of the Israeli Policy towards East Jerusalem.* Jerusalem: Center for Legal Aid and Human Rights.

Heller, Mark and Sari Nusseibeh (1991). *No Trumpets, No Drums: A Two-states Settlement to the Israeli Palestinian Conflict.* New York: Hill and Waag.

Kahanoff, Maya, S. Walid, R. Nasrallah and Y. Neumann (2007). *An Evaluation of Cooperation Between Palestinian and Israeli NGOs: An Assessment.* Geneva: UNESCO International Peace and Cooperation Center.

Kaufman, E., S. Walidet and J. Verhoeven (2006). *Bridging the Divide: Peacebuilding in the Israeli Palestinian Conflict.* Boulder, CO: Lynne Reinner Publishers.

Kelman, H. and J. Segal (2014). "New vision and strategies for a sustainable solution to the Israeli-Palestinian Conflict." Herbert C. Kelman Institute. Accessed at: http://kelmaninstitute.org/new-visions-and-strategies-for-a-sustainable-solution-to-the-israeli-palestinian-conflict/.

Lederach, John Paul (2003). *The Little Book of Conflict Transformation.* Brattleboro, VT: Good Books.

Middle East Monitor (2016). Israeli report: More than 400,000 settlers in West Bank, February 19, 2016. Accessed at: https://www.middleeastmonitor.com/20160219-israeli-report-more-than-400000-settlers-in-west-bank/

Qurie'a, Ahmad (2006a). *Camp David, Taba and Stockholm Negotiations 1995–2000*. Ramallah: Institute of Palestine Studies.

Qurie'a, Ahmad (2006b). *The Full Palestine Story of Negotiations, from Oslo to the Road Map, Oslo Negotiations 1995*. Ramallah: Institute of Palestine Studies.

Qurie'a, Ahmad (2014). *Annapolis Negotiation 2007–2008*. Ramallah: Institute of Palestine Studies.

Ramsbotham, Oliver, T. Woodhouse, and H. Miall (2008). *Contemporary Conflict Resolution*, 2nd Edition. Cambridge: Polity Press.

Ravid, Barak (2014). "Point of Departure?" *Haaretz Special Magazine for the Israel Conference on Peace*. July: 14–17.

Roy, Sara (2011). *Hamas and Civil Society in Gaza: Engaging the Islamic Social Sector*. Princeton, NJ: Princeton University Press.

Said, Edward (2001). *The End of the Peace Process, Oslo and After*. New York: Vintage Books.

Salem, Walid (2007). "Third-Party Involvement in the Israeli-Palestinian Conflict: A Quest for Peace-Building", in Kobi Michael and David Kellen, editors, *Stabilizing the Israeli-Palestinian Conflict*. Jerusalem: Harry Truman Research Institute for the Advancement of Peace.

Salem, Walid (2010). *Jerusalem Minority Report and a Human Security Community Based Agenda for the Change*. Jerusalem: The Center for Democracy and Community Development (CDCD).

Salem, Walid (2017). "Two-states solution and beyond: Can a federative/confederative solution work for Palestine/Israel?" (unpublished paper).

Sayigh, Yezid (1995). "Redefinition of the basics: Life and security for the Palestinian State." *Palestinian Studies Journal* 22: 12–31.

Segal, Jerome (2012). *Establishing UNSCOP and Step 2 at the* UN. Accessed at: http://www.miftah.org/Doc/PolicyPapers/UNSCOP-Annex.pdf.

Shaath, Nabil (2006). "Refugees in Taba Negotiations." Faculty of Law, Al Quds University, international conference on Palestinian refugee conditions and recent developments, November 2006.

Sheleff, Leon (2005). *The Thin Green Line: From Intractable Problem to Feasible solution in the Israeli Palestinian Conflict*. Bloomington, IN: Xlibris Corporation.

Solomon, Jay (2009). "Interview with Khaled Mashal." *The Wall Street Journal*, July 31. Accessed at: www.wsj.com.

Spears, Ian (2014). "Evaluating the two-state condominialism: A new approach to resolving the Israeli-Palestinian conflict?" *Global Change, Peace and Security Journal* 26, 2.

The Palestinian National Authority (2012). *Equitable Development: Moving forward despite the occupation*. The PNA position paper to the Ad Hoc Liaison Committee, Brussels.

Trump, Donald (1987). *The Art of the Deal*. New York: Ballantine Books.

United Nations Office of the Coordination of the Humanitarian Affairs, Occupied Palestinian Territory (2011). *Displacement and Insecurity in Area C of the West Bank*.

www.ingramcontent.com/pod-product-compliance
Lightning Source LLC
Chambersburg PA
CBHW031328230926
51848CB00001B/136
* 9 7 8 9 0 0 4 3 9 3 2 8 8 *